T0015514

A Pagan Polemic

A PAGAN POLEMIC

Reflections on Nature, Consciousness, and Anarchism

Jack Loeffler

University of New Mexico Press | Albuquerque

ISBN 978-0-8263-6517-0 (paper)
ISBN 978-0-8263-6518-7 (electronic)

Library of Congress Cataloging-in-Publication data is on file with the Library of
Congress

Founded in 1889, the University of New Mexico sits on the traditional homelands of the
Pueblo of Sandia. The original peoples of New Mexico—Pueblo, Navajo, and Apache—
since time immemorial have deep connections to the land and have made significant
contributions to the broader community statewide. We honor the land itself and those
who remain stewards of this land throughout the generations and also acknowledge our
committed relationship to Indigenous peoples. We gratefully recognize our history.

Cover photograph by Jack Loeffler
Designed by Felicia Cedillos
Composed in Adobe Caslon Pro 10.25/14

This book is dedicated to Katherine,
my beloved mate through the decades.
Adiós, Catalina, compañera de mi vida.

Contents

Prologue. Rambling Reflections of the Reservoir of Memory   ix

1. | Our Window: An Editorial—1972   1

2. | The Practice of Aural History   4

3. | Native Windows into the Natural World   14

4. | Aldo Leopold in the Southwest   26

5. | Averting Dystopia   35

6. | LUCA's Dream   41

7. | Conflicting Ideologies   46

8. | Counterculture in the Land of Clear Light   52

9. | In Praise of Restoration Ecology   71

10. | Nature Abhors a Maximum   80

11. | A Sonoran Illumination   86

12. | Thinking Like a Watershed   91

13. | The Colorado River Compact Is 100 Years Old   96

14. | On Direct Action   118

15. | A Case for Naturist Anarchism   122

16. | Naturizing Consciousness   128

17. | Seeking Coherence   134

18. | Lingering Speculations   139

Conclusion. | Invigorating Metamorphosis   145

Acknowledgments   151

Prologue

Rambling Reflections on the Reservoir of Memory

When I was about twelve years old living with my parents in an apartment complex adjacent to the Cheney estates in Manchester, Connecticut, I had something of a vision. I was alone on a Sunday morning looking past the pine trees into the beautiful, uncluttered emptiness of rolling grassland estates maintained by the Cheney family. I was suddenly overwhelmed by the beauty and imbued with a deep sense of the spirit of place that lasted for some time. That may well have marked those first moments when an entirely different level of perception swept me out of my former frame of reference wrought by a system of cultural biases, and into my own stream of consciousness. On further reflection, I realize that I've been running the rapids of my own stream of consciousness ever since. That early experience would have occurred in 1948, or thereabouts, when post–World War II Americans were delighting in a newfound level of overabundance after suffering the Great Depression followed by the war. At that time, the human population of the planet had yet to reach three billion. For those of us born east of the hundredth meridian, the West was still regarded as wild.

I longed to head west but was thwarted by circumstances of youth for seven more years until I was claimed by the US Army and landed in the Mojave Desert as an Army bandsman. By then I had decided to leave college to become an ignominious drifter by family standards. Yet I felt that I was being true to myself. Granted, I was wearing a uniform in a military band, but was one of a group of several fellow jazz musicians who jammed incessantly and even played gigs for the coin of the realm, thus greatly improving our fiscal status. Two years after having been drafted, I was honorably released from active duty and was finally truly free to wander through the rest of my life as I saw fit.

So just where is all this leading? It's been nearly three quarters of a century since my first mystical moment gazing into the Cheney estates. I have since wandered many thousands of miles either with or without purpose—by pick-up truck, by foot, or by raft. I now live in a mostly rural part of northern New Mexico. I luxuriate in the flow of Nature and try assiduously to remain unencumbered by those same cultural biases that I escaped long ago. However, those same cultural biases have become ever more deeply imbued in monocultural consciousness to the point that unless we shed them in the light of present reality, we go down.

I'd like to examine some of these institutional biases starting with organized religion. Many of the nearly eight billion humans inhabiting planet Earth abide by religious principles founded on mythic moments thousands of years old, first propounded by visionaries whose visions have been ever reinterpreted by less gifted individuals, themselves fenced in by frames of reference designed more to thwart than release the spirit within. Or so it seems to me. I was once asked to leave a mandatory college Bible class when responding to the professor's query. I responded by saying that I found the Bhagavad Gita considerably more interesting and compelling than the Bible. That's a simplistic example, but it reflects what I'm trying to convey. Basically, we crystallize ethereal visions into systems of rote to fit within preconceived often erroneous ideas of reality. I hearken back to Albert Einstein who regarded himself as a spiritual being who abhorred religiosity. I had long ago lost any modest interest in Christianity, actually about the time I had a mystical vision looking into the beautiful Cheney estates when my natural paganistic proclivities began to foment in earnest.

I found myself reading the Tao Te Ching at age twenty-four while sitting on a ledge overlooking the Pacific Ocean in Big Sur. I think that that small book is a work of profound merit. It is often attributed to Lao Tzu, ostensibly a retired Chinese archivist some 2,500 or so years ago, five centuries before Christ, eight centuries after Moses. In no way am I a religious scholar, but I've modestly delved into some of the world's religions earlier on. I have friends who became deeply involved in Zen Buddhism, a practice for which I have great respect. But for myself, I've long since taken my cue from the flow of Nature. I've always loved being "out in it," watching, sensing, listening, intuiting, registering Nature's great revelations. Thus, although I've largely avoided labeling myself, I've come to think of myself simply as a "naturist," an expansive term used earlier in reference to nudists.

In an earlier time, I would have been regarded as a pagan, to me an honorable epithet, and thus I named this modest tome, *A Pagan Polemic*. There are several definitions of the word *pagan*, and they all express Nature as an aspect of paganism. Coincidentally, I have a late distant relative named Charles Martin Loeffler who was both a violinist who served as assistant concert master with the Boston Symphony Orchestra, and a composer, one of whose compositions is titled "A Pagan Poem." The flow of Nature runs deep through our species, if we would but listen to its song.

As I have recorded many traditional Indigenous peoples throughout the West about their perspectives, the importance of Nature and the sacredness of homeland have remained as predominant leitmotifs throughout. I personally find my intuitive sensibilities to be far more in tune with the perspectives of these Indigenous peoples, and far less with the system of cultural attitudes expressed by much of mainstream American culture. As I grow older, I find myself ever more polemical in my environmentalism. Thus, after long consideration, I decided to title this anthology of essays *A Pagan Polemic* in the hope that readers will grasp the deep wisdom that is enshrined in the perspectives of so many traditional Indigenous peoples whose recorded interviews I have excerpted for this offering. I have also provided excerpts from recorded conversations with others, including writers and scientists and those whose perspectives provide glimpses into their own lives and thoughts. Several of these people have become true friends who share my love of the natural world.

I try very hard NOT to anthropomorphize, but rather see things for what they are without preconceived notions about anything. I admit to having a bias of interpreting things either as natural or unnatural. It could well be argued that humans are born of Nature and thus natural, but I counter by saying that humans are capable of unnatural acts, unnatural points of view. Certainly, we have overproliferated, overindulged, and collectively try to master Nature as our God-given right. The coldest temperature I've experienced is about -30 degrees Fahrenheit, the warmest about 120 degrees Fahrenheit. Those are extremes. However, I've read, but am yet to verify, that the absolute coldest it can be is -459.67 degrees Fahrenheit, and the absolute hottest is estimated to be 2.566×10^{33} degrees Fahrenheit. So, we who live within the present biotic community here on planet Earth survive within a tiny temperature range within the enormity of possibility.

This planet is our natural habitat. This planet, in conjunction with the Sun, spawned us and every other species that has ever lived here over the last 3.8 billion years. We are part of the flow of Nature as experienced on our home planet, Earth. No other place in the universe can possibly be as welcoming. Just to set the matter into some greater perspective, there are estimated to be at least two hundred billion stars in our home galaxy that we call the Milky Way. Some astronomers and cosmologists estimate there to be as many as 200 billion or more galaxies in the knowable universe. The universe ostensibly popped into being some 13.8 billion solar years ago in an event known as "the Big Bang." Where did THAT come from? Certainly not from an anthropomorphic god. There is much that is unknowable. Such is the nature of the Great Mystery.

Thus, organized religions are far from sufficient to serve us well. To my mind, only Nature in its broadest sense contains answers and insights into absolute reality. And from that point of view, Nature, alone is sufficient to serve all aspects within our universe.

But what is the nature of other possible universes?

Here we are, a species with a level of consciousness capable of perceiving an ever-greater sense of the wholeness of reality. We have "paltrified" this gift of consciousness on too many fronts. Rather than living up to our potential, we are squandering the resources necessary for life as we know it to continue to linger here on our home planet.

That's the rub.

There are many ways that we have created biases for ourselves. Take politics, for example. Ed Abbey pointed out that politics mainly serves the interests of those who govern. He also pointed out that money provides power, and in Ed's estimation, power is the root of all evil. These days, political power reigns within every nation, and here in America, corporate economics fuels political power.

Ever since the end of World War II, corporate economics has become a force of enormous magnitude. I won't say a force of Nature, because to me, economics in its current incarnation of pursuing "growth for the sake of growth," is "unnatural." Why is it unnatural? Simplistically because unbounded endless growth inevitably results in depletion of finite natural resources. That we pursue this, while recognizing and ably extrapolating the ramifications, is intensifying likelihood for the end of life of those species who rely on finite resources for survival. We are one among those species, yet we do it anyway. This has resulted in a particularly fatal economically driven political bias that governs modern America and beyond. This has been evident for some time, yet we have not succeeded in thwarting either this bias or its lethal practice.

Becoming addicted to drugs can be lethal for the individual. Getting hooked on money and power can result in extinction of our own species as well as many others.

What about racial bias? Prejudice in any form is insidious. Prejudice against "otherness" has prevailed for thousands of years. Egyptians enslaved Hebrews. East Indians continue to prevail within a sharply defined caste system. From the point of view of at least some Christians, any non-Christian is doomed to the fires of Hell. Former

US president Donald Trump having spurred on right-wing constituents, constructed an enormous wall to keep Mexicans and others out of America. This has resulted in metaphorically walling off anything that seems different or alien in any way. White-skinned people have disastrously held sway over anyone darker-skinned in America and elsewhere. Skin color is a dividing characteristic misunderstood as racial differentiation. The study of genetics has revealed that we *Homo sapiens* are a single species regardless of skin tone. Present-day humans are no longer divided into different species. However, many of us contain Neanderthal or Denisovan genes, which was only recently discovered. As a white dude of European ancestry, I may possess as much as 2 percent Neanderthal in my genetic makeup, whereas Black folks of African descent are unlikely to possess any Neanderthal in their genetic makeup. When I was growing up, Neanderthals were considered inferior beings relative to *Homo sapiens*. By that measure, I'm inferior to my Black cousins who are *Homo sapiens* to the core.

"Racial" prejudice is based on fear of other-ness. Conversely, I admit to being deeply biased against many politicians and their financiers. I am not exempt from bias, but I'm surely particularly selective based on eighty-five years of observation.

———

BOTTOM LINE HERE is that there's a good chance that all species alive today on our planet Earth are descended from a last universal common ancestor (LUCA). LUCA was but a single-celled entity, possibly born near a hydrothermal vent in an ancient ocean. There were earlier living cells, but ostensibly their lineages died off. LUCA, however, was apparently tough enough to endure, and even reproduce, to become our great-grandparent to the umpteenth power whose lineage includes by some estimates over five billion distinct fellow species, depending on how the term "species" is interpreted. Just think of that! Every time I look at the great juniper tree outside the west window of my studio, I recognize my kindred-ness with that tree. Its body, like my own, is itself an ecosystem within the greater ecosystem, thus home to many species and visited by many more. Not long ago, I watched a bobcat eat a prairie dog beneath that tree and was deeply moved by witnessing yet another aspect of the flow of Nature.

To me, Nature spawns everything in the universe and is evolving all-encompassing procedure herein. But what spawned Nature? Or has Nature always existed in many guises depending on the nature of the "multiverse"? That is beyond even the most imaginative speculation to grasp.

When I look into the night sky over northern New Mexico with my ancient eyes, I see at least two thousand stars on a clear night and the vaguest hint of another galaxy known as Andromeda to be found near the constellation, Cassiopeia. Andromeda is located about 2.5 million light years away and is ostensibly destined to collide with our Milky Way Galaxy four or five billion years hence. So, no immediate worries concerning Andromeda. But it certainly would be interesting to witness the collision.

Back here on Earth, we have far more immediate worries: climate change, pandemic, human overpopulation, ubiquitous pollution, dwindling nonrenewable natural resources, and to me the most profound, intertwined systems of errant human attitudes too deeply ensconced in various biases to successfully shift into a more holistic perspective. This by itself is an existential threat.

Part of me remains optimistic, however, that may be the nature of my chemical and mental makeup. It is also partly founded on learning of those young people who are working hardcore environmentalists, folks who spend time in the field, rather than offices, who actually get outside and work and play. I am deeply grateful to these folks who persevere relentlessly, who have escaped the cruel shackles of the spirit born of an economically dominated paradigm, who realize that the flow of Nature is where the real action is. Skinny-dipping in the flow of Nature is one of life's greatest, most essential joys.

I was young sixty years ago, associated with the Beat scene of the Bay Area until I realized that I needed to be in the rural high country of the Southwest. Earlier on, I'd hitchhiked across the country and was spellbound by New Mexico. Thus, I moved to New Mexico and have remained here ever since. I camped throughout the 1960s, living in different forests, or deserts, trekking endlessly around the Colorado Plateau. At one point, I lived in a three-forked-stick hogan near the base of Navajo Mountain for half a year. For three annual seasons, I was a fire lookout atop Caracas Mesa in northwestern New Mexico where I lived outside a hundred days and nights a year. Camping was my way of life.

In 1973, my wife, Katherine, and I built our own handcrafted adobe home on the upstream edge of Santa Fe, and there remained until it became too crowded. We sold our handcrafted house and acquired another adobe home fifteen miles out of town in a rural countryside where we've lived ever since. After twenty-seven years, it has become my favorite campsite, and I content myself in my old age by walking through this region every morning and spending part of everyday outside immersing myself in the flow of Nature.

Looking back, I've been blessed by circumstance to have met and befriended many people of various cultural persuasions who have allowed me to record their own perspectives. This has resulted in an aural history archive that has contributed to and helped sustain my own reservoir of memory. Almost every word, every song, every birdcall, every sound that I've ever recorded is preserved and archived for posterity in a collection that I've donated to the History Museum of New Mexico at the Palace of the Governors in Santa Fe. Northern New Mexico has remained the homeland that I've ever returned to from countless adventures throughout the American West, Mexico, and far beyond.

Perhaps the remotest place I have ever been to was the tiny atoll called Rarotonga in the Cook Islands in the South Pacific where, nearly fifty years ago, I spent a month as part of a film crew documenting Maori creation myths celebrated in ceremonials as a joint project of the Smithsonian Institution and National Geographic Society. These ceremonials were performed by different populations of

Maori people who live throughout the Cook Islands and elsewhere. And it was there that the extraordinary influence that environment has on cultural evolution was verified for me yet again through the Maori practice of their mythic process. The Maori people are masters of navigation, aptly demonstrated by their having populated so many islands in the South Pacific, traveling by outrigger canoes long before the mapping of the oceans by Western cartographers.

In the main, I've remained within the North American Southwest, the paradise wherein I feel most spiritually attuned. I love it all—the four great American deserts, the Colorado Plateau, the mountains, the watersheds, the myriad campsites—and the perspectives of other folks be they Native American, Hispano, Gringo or otherwise. I've camped throughout this homeland. My camping compañero for decades was author Ed Abbey, and he shared his unique wit and wisdom with me in endless conversation around campfires or as we walked literally for thousands of miles throughout this most arid region of our continent. Katherine's and my daughter, Celestia Peregrina, has also been a great camping partner and fellow river runner.

My family and close friendships remain central to my life. In this slender tome, I've included some excerpts from conversations that continue to enrich that reservoir of memory that comes with what I call *octogenarianismo*. It is an honor to be over eighty years old. Many of these essays were earlier published in different periodicals, including *Green Fire Times*, *El Palacio* magazine, *Wild Earth* magazine, *The Gulch*, and *Earth Island Journal*, over a period of fifty years.

Most importantly, I have this to say: my heart and love and respect pour forth to those young people who are working so diligently, so relentlessly on behalf of the health of our planet Earth, whose deep calling is to save us from ourselves. This modest offering is for you with my deepest gratitude. Thank you.

A PAGAN POLEMIC

1. | Our Window

An Editorial—1972

This essay originally appeared in Clear Creek *(1972)*.

IN 1965, I TOOK a job as a fire lookout in a remote corner of the Southwest known as Cedar Rock. Long before the US Forest Service had come into existence, "the Rock" was used as a lookout by Indians looking for other Indians, or perhaps for some sign of the Great Spirit. Somehow, after sitting on top of the Rock for months at a time—marking the place where the Sun rose and set, listening to the songs of coyotes and wild turkeys, seeing the dance of lightning bolts across the forest and beyond, and one day watching two golden eagles mysteriously hovering overhead for an hour—I became filled with a profound sense of awe and deep reverence for the flow of Nature.

Each year after I left the lookout, the contentment would remain for a while. But as I participated more and more in the world of the twentieth century, my sensitivities acquired callouses, and that vision from the Rock became the memory that kept me going. It is always with me, but I am rarely there.

There are lots of folks who share that vision—who seek it in the forests of Mendocino or on the beaches of the Sea of Cortez or perhaps in age-long ceremonials such as the Hopis and Navajos perform. But there are many more of us who rarely have the chance to look deeply into the eye of the Earthmother.

We know we are in trouble now. Modern Western culture has centralized, compacted itself in great metropolitan centers from which it is difficult to see the image of the mountain. As we separate ourselves from the flow of Nature by concrete and techno-fantasy, we begin to see ourselves only through our own eyes and deeds. Our point of view has become anthropocentric to the extent that we have forgotten that, indeed, we are part of the biospheric process. As a result, we have grown to rely on mass production of what we are taught to think we need instead of relying on ourselves. Our lives are not handcrafted. We do not walk in beauty. And we have created a juggernaut, a crisis of energy expenditure to support our techno-fantasy that threatens the Earth. Our technological prowess has become the end rather than the means. Donella and Dennis Meadows's work (*The Limits to Growth*) shows that the computer, the icon of our techno-fantastic world has said, in essence: STOP. THE PROCESS CAN NO LONGER CONTINUE OR SEVERE CRISIS IS IMMINENT. But how can we stop?

Many, perhaps most of us are not convinced that we must now achieve a nongrowth point of view. To live within a steady state system and use a basic minimum technology is counter to the very precepts of Western culture.

If there is no solution, what can we do?

We must create a model of solution. Today, the Southwest, with all its beauty and diversity, is condemned to be exploited for its natural resources to support the juggernaut of modern Western culture. The Southwest contains coal reserves intended to fire power plants, which will in turn provide more power for the metropolitan areas of the Pacific Southwest. To the Bureau of Reclamation, the Southwest is a momentary answer to the energy needs of the West. To the traditional Indians, to many non-Indians who live there or visit there, the Southwest is the last refuge of peace, beauty, and natural balance.

It is not necessary that the Southwest be sacrificed now. If we, as a culture, accept the Southwest as our symbol of environmental integrity—if we deeply, yet consciously recognize the tragic folly of desecrating the Southwest and simply do not allow that to happen— we will once again evoke in the mind's eye of American culture the image of the mountain. And we will know the intrinsic meaning of a bioethic. We will have a positive symbol of a solution to our dilemma.

It will take tremendous effort to reverse this juggernaut that threatens the Southwest. It will involve every one of us. We must look deep inside ourselves for the sensitivities and sensibilities that will allow us to *know* what we can do. Saving the Southwest will teach us how to separate our needs from our wants. It will provide insight into what sort of education our children really need if they are to survive. Most important, we will learn, once again, the meaning of ethics, of bioethics, and what is truly demanded of us if the Earth and her creatures are to continue in *our* present form.

2. | The Practice of Aural History

The practice of aural history involves the disciplines
of systems thinking and listening to the commons.

I FIRST TURNED ON a tape recorder in 1958. It was a Webcor, and
I was making a monaural recording of our jazz quintet for a demo. I
immediately realized the enormous potential of recording sound—not
just music but every kind of sound. The recorder is to hearing what the
camera is to seeing. For most humans at least, sound and sight are the
two most registered of the five bodily senses. And while sight may well
be the more consistently captivating, I consider sound to be the most
deeply penetrating of the senses, and as such, an enormous contributor
to memory and cognition, hence the wellspring of many higher levels
of consciousness. Thus, for the last half-century, a sound recorder has
been the keystone artifact in my kit, which also includes microphones,
a modest camera, notebook, pen, and canteen.

The North American Southwest is the heartland of my greater territory that also includes the contiguous United States west of the hundredth meridian, as well as northwestern Mexico. I have followed my
microphones throughout this span of landscape recording habitats
and individual animal species including the human species. I've
recorded thunder, flowing water, wind passing through ponderosa
pine forest, cottonwood trees, and quaking aspen. I've recorded insects
buzzing, rattlesnakes rattling, horses farting, crickets rasping—even
stomachs growling. I've recorded thousands of songs rendered by

Indigenous peoples throughout this region, hundreds of stories, thoughts, perspectives of shamans, hunter-gatherers, tillers of the soil, writers of books, scientists, environmentalists, counterculturalists, politicians, political activists, poets, corporate hierarchs, fisher-folk, salt-of-the earth. And I've recorded many dozens of musical concerts ranging through medieval, renaissance, baroque, classical, and modern compositions performed by professional musicians, often of the highest caliber. I have followed my microphones through my fields of fascination and have created what I call my aural history archive. Thanks to digitization, I can pull up each of my individual recordings from over the last five decades whether it be a Seri Indian singing the song of the leafcutter ant, a flock of sandhill cranes in their sunrise flight in search of food, the night song of the Mexican wolf, Mahler's fourth symphony performed by Santa Fe Pro Musica, or *Las cantigas d'amigo* composed by Martin Codax, the thirteenth century Galician jongleur. I am instantly transported back to when I made each recording and can fairly recall the conditions of the moment. My imagination is vigorously reawakened through the practice of aural history in such manner as to collapse time and thus perceive my life as an integrated system of consciousness.

Indeed, my life as a self-employed aural historian remains a continuing span of adventure, intellectually and intuitively fascinating, aesthetically satisfying. Thus, I may listen yet again to the late white-water adventurer Martin Litton addressing future restoration of Glen Canyon in the wake of construction of the Glen Canyon Dam on the Colorado River that submerged an exquisite habitat beneath the waters of Lake Powell in the early 1960s: "The Colorado River causes me a little less worry when you consider the fate of its canyons because we know that the dams are temporary. But human use, enjoyment, and inspiration of what those dams have affected and what they have damaged, are things we have lost in our lifetime. We won't see restoration of Glen Canyon. Still, there's a strong movement that's even nobler because of that—to go after the restoration of something which we can't utilize when it is restored because we won't be here. A movement of that kind that is far-reaching. Looking ahead, as the Glen Canyon Institute does, and the Glen Canyon Action Network ... seems to me to have a kind of nobility of purpose. I won't be able to use it. I won't have fun there. I'll never see it, but maybe my descendants will. The glens for which Glen Canyon was named will come back, perhaps—the oaks and so forth that Major Powell was so enthralled by."

I recorded that conversation with Martin Litton from which I excerpted the above on April 28, 2001. I was in the throes of producing a six-part radio series entitled *Moving Waters: The Colorado River and the West* for Public Radio. This was my attempt to create a larger perspective using aural history to invigorate a perception of the entire watershed of the Colorado River as an integrated system rather than simply a source of water for both agriculture and the urban Southwest. Additionally, I've come to regard Martin Litton and his close friend David Brower as cofounders of the modern environmental movement by having engaged the Sierra Club in thwarting the construction of two dams on the Green River, the chief tributary of the Colorado River, dams that would have flooded Dinosaur National Monument.

I have enormous respect for my Native American friends of myriad cultural persuasions who still tend to their ancient traditions and vigorously attempt to stay the juggernaut of mainstream monoculture that would subsume their homelands for purposes of extraction of natural resources. These are peoples who have been shaped in part by their respective habitats, for whom the land and its denizens remain sacred, many of whom still consider themselves as part of the wildlife. Over the decades, I have conducted recorded interviews, conversations, songs, and events with Indigenous peoples from as far north as the Nez Perce Indians for whom the watershed of the Clearwater River is homeland, to as far south as the Río Chapalagana watershed in the Sierra Madre Occidental, homeland to the Huichol Indians. I've also recorded the habitats of many of these native peoples, and later on as I have produced scores of radio programs and sound collages in my studio in rural New Mexico, I lay down a stereo sound bed of the ambient sounds of peoples' specific homelands over which I have mixed in excerpts from my recordings of their interviews. In this way, I have attempted to subliminally suggest that the human voice is but one of many in any natural landscape.

Lilian Hill is a young Hopi woman whom I've had the honor to befriend who was willing to share her cultural perspective with me regarding her place in Nature:

"Within the songs that we learn when we're really young or that we're exposed to, a lot of the songs talk about the relationship that the Earth has to the clouds, that the clouds have with different animals, and things like that. And one of the ways we describe the Earth is as a woman, or as our Mother, and that's how we treat Her and how we believe in Her. And so the word that we use even in our songs is *tuwakatsi*, and what that means is the life of the soil, the life of the land is not without recognition. It's alive, it's a living being. It has a really deep meaning because the way that we learn these things is in the context of songs."

I've come to realize that music is a powerful mnemonic device that often adheres culture to homeland. Many songs mimic the sounds of natural habitat. And beyond that, I've come to realize that the mythic process itself is a means through which cultures of habitat intuitively define their reason to be within their place in Nature.

One of the great lore-masters of our time is my friend Camillus Lopez who is a member of the Tohono O'odham Independent Nation. I've recorded Camillus on several occasions, and each time he has provided a deep insight into the sacred nature of the Earth and her habitats:

"To learn a thing, you have to learn to respect things. If you don't respect things, it's just because you never learned it somewhere. So to those people that are there just for themselves, they have to learn how to respect things. Because if they don't it affects everybody.

"There's Baboquivari. That's where I'itoi [the mischief making creator] lives. That's what's sacred about it. But in the O'odham culture every mountain is sacred. Every mountain has its story. When you share a song about that mountain, you don't say it's any better than that other mountain. There's no levels, no degrees to more sacred or less sacred. It's that every mountain, every little sand, every wash is sacred. It has a story behind it. That's why it was made. If there was no reason for it to be there, it would not have been made. So every mountain has its sacredness."

Both Lilian Hill and Camillus Lopez were born into ancient cultures native to the North American Southwest. Humans are known to have ranged this region for at least twelve thousand years and perhaps even longer. Hunter-gatherers of yore have left profound evidence of their passage through the land with artifacts such as projectile points, potshards, petroglyphs, and pictographs rendered in wondrous rock art that reveal something of their cultural perspective. Many of the songs and stories are of ancient provenance, as are ceremonials, dances, and chants that transport the participants into states of consciousness that are deeply aligned with sacred homeland. The sound of the drumming and shaking of rattles that accompany the chanting and rhythmic stamping of feet is an aural experience of magnitude that reenacts mythic moments within the ceremonial and transforms the consciousness in the minds of the participants for whom the ceremonials have traditional meaning that extends into antiquity.

The traditional native peoples of this landscape are possessed of attitudes and levels of consciousness reflecting their place in Nature that seem to have largely atrophied in modern mainstream monoculture shaped more by the fruits of the Industrial Revolution, consumerism, and wavering religions founded on the notion of a transcendental god. Mastery, rather than collaboration, seems to be the primary cultural urge of the modern mind, whereas intuiting the realm of natural history is relegated to the sidelines.

One chilly day in 1986, I visited two-time Pulitzer Prize-winning author Paul Horgan in the home of his final years in Middletown, Connecticut. Horgan was by then an emeritus at Wesleyan University but continued to live on campus in the old carriage house. I recorded a conversation with him wherein I asked him to talk about two of his books, *Great River: The Río Grande in North American History* and *Lamy of Santa Fe*. Paul Horgan was perhaps the most erudite person I've ever come to know, and he remains in my memory as a friend whom I regard with greatest respect. At one point, I asked him to address the arrival of the Anglo in the New Mexico Territory, which at that time included much of northern Mexico:

"Of course, the very first motive was commercial, the coming of the Anglos. And though a not wholly ignoble motive, it certainly was a selfish one. Therefore, something of that emotional commitment to a purpose had enduring effect on all relationships that resulted between the occupants—namely the Indians and the Hispanos and the incoming Yankees, Anglos. I know that superior judgments were almost invariably rendered upon the inhabitants by those who came. For instance, Josiah Gregg, of whom I've written and who was himself a very interesting and useful, admirable person. Still, his judgment and others who came to Santa Fe early . . . saw what they saw as a squalid society. Well, it was different and it was simple and it was primitive, but it had its qualities of goodness and integrity, but it was alien. But it was the enormous power of the commercial interests—the mercantile interests which were the first to invade New Mexico and get established—that got the upper hand very fast because of their superior economic weight. And that endured—I suppose it still does—in numbers."

In the minds of those early Anglos, they were following their Manifest Destiny, their providential right to take over this continent regardless of the presence of millions of Indigenous people who had successfully inhabited their sacred homelands for countless generations. For the newcomers, this was a landscape rich in natural resources to be plundered for economic profit. And thus, they secularized the landscape and sought to stamp out the local deities, to eliminate the spirit of place. They came with the intent to privatize the commons— the water, the minerals, the forests, even the pelts of animals in order to increase personal wealth. As Horgan pointed out, while their motives may not have been entirely noble, they were certainly selfish, founded largely on greed. This condition continues to prevail.

Many years ago, I interviewed a young Navajo regarded as an outlaw by the federal powers that be, namely the culture that had created legislation in direct violation of natural law. There was a movement afoot in the halls of the US Congress to relocate up to ten thousand Navajos from their homeland that lies adjacent to the Hopi Nation of what is presently called Arizona. The young Navajo was working desperately to thwart this congressional move to open these Indian lands—homeland to thousands of Navajos for generations—for mineral extraction. He had become the proverbial "thorn in the side" of the feds.

Deep into our conversation, he regarded me with despair and asked, "Where does all that murderous thought come from?" I had no response to that.

The young outlaw's mother lived in her traditional hogan on Big Mountain, part of Black Mesa where she herded her sheep, the area where the feds were intent on moving the Navajos out. I met with her, and of a late afternoon, helped her herd her flock of sheep back to their corral. She invited me into her hogan, where I set up my recorder. This is part of what she said:

"This is where we're losing the whole area here. If we lose, where are we going to put our medicine? . . . Mainly this place is the big sacred spot right here. Where are they going to make a sand painting if they wanted to have prayers? Where are they going to put that in the [prayer] baskets? This is the main spot right here.

"We can't take these baskets or medicines on either side of these sacred mountains. This is a special spot. This is what they should talk about or should think of it. But this means that all these Big Mountains and Navajo Mountain are really sacred for the four sacred mountains. They're messengers. They sent words or news or something like that to these sacred mountains. Whatever is happening out here in these four sacred mountains, they sent words to these. There's a medicine man that uses prayers and this is the area where the winds send his message to these four main sacred mountains.

"This is how we always say we hate to have these mountains to be destroyed because it talks like us in their way. Just like the trees, when the wind, it breezes and you could hear the sounds of it. And even the grasses, the grasses or whatever the herbs are, it really makes noise. And they're talking to each other by whispering or they might be praying or they might be singing, it's the sound that we hear. If they're destroyed, we can't use any medicine out of it because we use medicine and foods. These plants are with us. Some are medicine, some are food, and if it's a real serious illness comes around to a person, then we use some strong herbs for it. And they're growing around among us.

"A lot of things have been planned on this area that's the mine or the uranium or the oil, whatever comes up, and they want to start destroying our medicines. This is the main point, that we can't give up. As long as I'm here, I'm not going to give up. According to our old ancestors, they said don't ever give up. There's something going to happen. It's going to be ruined someday. Either you're going to be shot or you're going to be destroyed first, and then they're going to destroy the land. So I think it's coming up near every day. It's what we've been thinking."

These interviews took place just forty years ago. Some Navajos were relocated, however, that old lady whom I interviewed never did give up. She died some time ago, but she still had her land and her sheep and her hogan with her rifle by the door. I loved that old lady whose name was Roberta Blackgoat, and I continue to hold her in highest esteem.

Twenty or so years after I recorded the young Navajo living in hiding from the feds, and his mother in her hogan, I recorded a Navajo *hataali*, or shaman, at Navajo Mountain, the remotest corner of Navajo homeland. His name is Herman Atine, and he shared something of his profoundly beautiful perspective:

"Everything here between the Earth, the Sun, the Moon is all related and is in the creation stories. Before humans—before we were made, there were only deities, spirits in this here world. They're part of being healthy for us; they're part of Nature that we have to use to get knowledge to take care of ourselves, our families, our relatives, and for our society. It's all part of it—the Sun, the Earth, the Moon. In our culture, we have the benefit of having it in our creation stories, and we can relate back to it to help us be better people, to acquire the knowledge that's related to it to function, to have respect for ourselves and everything else." He speaks his prayers to the wind that carries them to the four sacred mountains.

Not all European descendants are inclined to turn habitat into money. In my personal experience there are of those us who "resist much, obey little" as old Walt Whitman advised. There are many who sense the sacred quality in this Earth, who live in beauty as we walk through this land.

Some time ago, I conducted an enlightening interview with the great American author, Wendell Berry who said this to me:

"As for wild, I now think the word is misused. The longer I have lived and worked here among the noncommercial creatures of the woods and fields, the less I've been able to conceive of them as wild. They plainly are going about their own domestic lives, finding or making shelter, gathering food, minding their health, raising their young, always well-adapted to their places. They are far better at domesticity than we industrial humans are. It became clear to me also that they think of us as wild and that they are right. We are the ones who are undomesticated, barbarous, unrestrained, disorderly, extravagant, and out of control. They are our natural teachers and we have learned too little from them."

Wendell Berry is indeed a wise man, a man of the Earth. Native American folk have learned much from our fellow creatures who inhabit the deserts, the mountains, the forests, the prairies, the watersheds of our planet. As an aural historian, a wanderer who loves to listen to the different voices in our earthly biotic community, I have heard balance and harmony in Nature's chorus—that is until I step into civilization where the song of the so-called "wild" is drowned out by the fruits of industry, the endless banter that prevails in this techno-fantastic creation of monocultural humankind.

That's why I, myself opt to live in a rural homeland of limited deeded acreage that is returning to a natural state after heavy overgrazing in a previous century. At night I continue to listen to the Indigenous creatures, but now without recording them. However, sometime in the near future, I'll record two Hispano folk musicians to complete their album of superbly performed songs, some of which adhere their own culture to their New Mexico homeland of twenty generations. I love this music. Indeed, I've recorded three thousand or more of these folksongs. In so doing, I have gleaned some understanding of their culture, one that is blended in some measure with their Native American neighbors whom I've also recorded. Thus, I have made enduring friendships that continually stir the reservoir of my memory.

The practice of aural history is not my profession but rather my lifeway. Now at age eighty-five, I've all but stopped recording, but I listen incessantly. In large measure, this is the way I learn and remain alert. Just now, I heard the lookout call of the scaled quail, a summer denizen in my homeland. This year, I haven't heard the song of a meadowlark, a song that I formerly listened to with great delight every year. I hear Chihuahuan ravens almost continually. They are "wildly" intelligent. I hear fewer hawks over these last years. I love hawks of every species. Once I saw an aplomado falcon and drove into a ditch in my excitement. I try to see as much as I can as well as listen. We're gifted by Nature these five senses as well as our emotions, instincts, our intellect and our intuition.

We must not allow our intuition to continue to atrophy. In my opinion, it is perhaps the most important of the characteristics of human consciousness. By listening to our intuition, we may yet hear the grasses and the leaves in the trees carrying messages of life to the mountains that sustain the watersheds of our homelands, of ourselves.

3. | Native Windows into the Natural World

This essay originally appeared in Green Fire Times (2011).

"IT'S TECHNOLOGY THAT MEDIATES our experience of nature: TV wildlife programs, online games such as FarmVille, in which players plant and harvest virtual crops, digital projections of woodfires and skies for our homes, robotic dogs and electronic pets such as Tamagotchi. Technological nature is becoming increasingly sophisticated and pervasive. At the same time, we're destroying Nature very fast. These trends are transforming our existence." So said psychologist Peter Kahn, author and faculty member at the University of Washington, Seattle, in an interview in *New Scientist* magazine. Kahn also described an experiment that he and his colleagues conducted wherein people whose work rooms had a window to the out-of-doors recovered from stress significantly faster and more completely than those without windows, or even those whose monitors reflected digital displays of the natural world.

In other words, virtual reality is no substitute for the real McCoy—at least not yet, or until we allow techno-fantasy to subsume our proclivities to perform as natural beings within the flow of Nature. I cannot imagine a ghastlier fate for a natural species—the human species—with our capacity for consciousness and intuition. I admit that I have used my computer on a daily basis to edit classical music, and produce radio programs and sound collages for museums, to write essays and even the occasional book. But three feet to the left of my computer screen is a massive window that looks out over ten thousand square miles of northern New Mexico homeland. Four feet to right of that window is a door beyond which is a funky flagstone patio where, seated on my canvas camp chair, I have contemplated countless hours of daytime and nighttime delight in the flow of Nature as can only be rendered in the high, dry savannah of my homeland. Ten feet from my chair is a trailhead into that vastness into which I've wandered afoot for thousands of miles.

I am among the most fortunate of men. I have spent over two thirds of my still-lengthening life in immediate proximity to people of many different cultural persuasions, from midwestern nightclubs where I was a performing jazz musician—often the only ofay in the group—to a Navajo hogan, to a Hopi kiva, to a Huichol *kalihue*, to a Ute peyote teepee, to Tarahumara caves in the Barranca del Cobre, to the homes of myriad Native Americans and traditional Hispanos throughout the American West and beyond where I have found deep friendship, listened to stories and songs that reflect profound understanding of the flow of Nature. And I have come to understand that cultural diversity born largely of biological and geophysical diversity is a most valuable but greatly endangered element that characterizes our species.

Years ago, I recorded my late friend, cultural anthropologist Edward T. "Ned" Hall addressing this very issue:

"The land and the community are associated with each other. And the reason they're associated and linked, and the reason that people get their feeling of community from the land is that they all share in the land. Ethnicity is looked upon normally as a liability because people want to make everyone else like themselves. And this is something we're going to have to learn to overcome, because ethnicity is one of the greatest resources if not THE greatest resource that we have in the world today. What we have here are stored solutions to common human problems, and no one solution is ever going to work for over a long period time, so we need multiple solutions for these problems. So ethnicity is like money in the bank, but in a world bank. Culture is an extension of the genetic code. In other words, we are part of Nature ourselves. And one of the rules of Nature is that in order to have a stable environment, you have to have one that is extraordinarily rich and diverse. If you get it too refined, it becomes more vulnerable. So we need diversity in order to have insurance for the future. Again, you need multiple solutions to common problems. The evolution of the species really depends on not developing our technology but developing our spirits or our souls. The fact is that Nature is so extraordinarily complex that you can look at it from multiple dimensions, and come up with very different answers, and each one of them will be true. And we need all of those truths."

Ned Hall was on the mark.

———

THE SONORAN DESERT lies in the southwestern corner of the North American continent and is regarded as possibly the most luxuriant desert in the world. Humans have roamed this landscape since the Pleistocene epoch, the last ice age when the Sonoran landscape was characterized more by piñon-juniper grassland than by the great columnar cacti that now vegetate this exquisite desert landscape.

The late Danny Lopez was a Tohono-O'odham lore-master and elder who spent much of his adult life working assiduously to restore cultural attitudes and practices among his people. These people, formerly known to the outside world as the Papago Indians, have culturally evolved, adapted, and flourished in their desert homeland despite the influx of descendants of Europeans who have infiltrated their home habitat. Here, Mr. Lopez speaks of the old ways of his people.

"My elderly mother used to tell us we have to be industrious because to be a good worker was something valuable in the old culture. Nobody likes a lazy person. To be a worker, you're useful to your community, to your family, and to yourself. To be an early riser has a very important value, to get things done and to not sleep late. In the summertime out here in the desert, you got up early to do many of your chores before it got too hot, and then you could rest later on. And you ask for good health because long ago people lived a healthy life. Their diet was healthy eating off the land. The animals we hunted—the rabbit, the pack rat, the mule deer, the javelina, the other animals that helped us survive—we didn't simply kill an animal. We killed for our survival. Some people used to say that when you killed the deer, you spoke to the deer spirit to tell why you make the kill so we as people can survive.

"One of the things we never bother is the owl. We have a lot of respect for the owl. People used to say in the old culture that when we die our spirit will come back in the form of the owl. Everybody respects the eagle. We too have that respect for the eagle. We say that it is the most powerful of all the bird people. The feathers are used for different things. A medicine man will keep a deer's tail for a curing ceremony. If we do something wrong to certain animals, we might get sick later on and would have to have a curing ceremony. The medicine man would use a deer tail, the owl feather, or even little carved figures to imitate the horny toad or other figures.

"As children we were told to leave certain things alone like the horny toad. We always had respect for the horny toad. We never picked it up. We just left it alone. Even like the woodpecker. We never bothered the woodpecker. They would scold us as children if we threw rocks at the saguaro like little kids do. They would say, 'Leave the person alone. You're hurting the person.' I didn't understand. I didn't know as a little kid, but now I know why they said that. Because there is a story about how the first saguaro came to be, came from a person.

"Even the rabbit—after we cook it and eat it, we're told to wash our hands for a certain reason. Things like that we have respect for. The things that we planted, we had to pray, we had to sing, we had to dance and do a ceremony to bring the rains. And that's why the saguaro fruit is very important because from the fruit we make the syrup. Each family donates some of the syrup to the ceremony house where this brew is made. I don't compare it to beer, it's not that potent. After it ferments and sits in the roundhouse for two days and two nights, we drink it. It's a ceremony we go through. Again, it's all the call for rain because the Earth needs the rain. The plants need the rain, the desert animals need the rain. And of course, we as people need the rain. When the rains came, the monsoons, that's when we planted. We got our water from the rains. We grew our squash, our beans, our corn. You see, all those things we ate back then, we were eating healthy, and we were active people. Before the coming of the horse, we walked, we ran across the desert, and we kept ourselves healthy that way by being very active and eating healthy. But through time that has changed."

———

EVEN THOUGH CULTURAL recollection is subject to the vagaries of each generation's interpretation of the past relative to the present, it's as though the land itself has a memory that serves as a mnemonic device for the prevailing biotic community. Near the west bank of the northern Río Grande east of the Jemez Mountain is situated the Tewa Pueblo of Santa Clara. The inhabitants of the pueblo are descended from ancestral Puebloans thought to have inhabited Chaco Canyon and other sites in the Four Corners region of the Southwest. In many ways, Tewa culture has been shaped by home habitat. The term "environmental determinism" is a paltry phrase in the face of generations of individual and cultural life within the high plateaus of the arid Southwest.

Rina Swentzell was born into the Santa Clara Pueblo and was shaped by her culture. She also holds advanced degrees in architecture and American studies. Her span of consciousness is enormous, and here she shares some of her reflections on homeland.

"The old ancestral people moved through this region for thousands of years. And the intimacy that they developed with the land, I think, is what has kept them going for so long in such a place. Even today, I think we have forgotten that what has helped our people survive for so long is that intimacy that we had with the land, with the place, with the rocks, the mountains. Part of that intimacy, of course, especially in this region, is to know where the water areas are. The water is seen as being absolutely important for life. Without it, creation doesn't happen. It is the semen of the father that keeps creation going. But the snaking water through this region, the Río Grande, and of course throughout all of Pueblo mythology, the lakes are very important. All water places are extremely important because without water we don't survive here. And it is so sparse that they have become very special places. They are also those places in which the energy of the world is very strong because they are also openings of places to go to the underworld, other levels of existence that are openings to the underworld. The Río Grande is a place that is also frightening to the Pueblo people. It is frightening because it comes with incredible power. The power. And that is why I think that we talk about the 'water-wind-breath,' because the power of all creation is there. And it can be in the wind, and certainly in the water, and especially in that strong-flowing water that we know. And the word in Tewa for Río Grande is O-son-gue, the large water place."

———

THE HOPI INDIANS inhabit three southern promontories of Black Mesa in what is now northern Arizona. Their village of Oraibi is nearly a thousand years old and is considered to be the oldest continuously inhabited village in what is presently the contiguous forty-eight United States. As remote and as deeply imbedded in cultural traditions as they are, the Hopis have been besieged by a monoculture intent on extracting mineral resources and water from their homeland. Their sense of connectedness to the land is ancient and runs deep. Phillip Tuwaletstiwa was born into traditional Hopi culture and was trained as a geodesist. For some time, he served as the assistant director of the National Geodetic Survey. He is a man who always knows where he is.

Phillip Tuwaletstiwa: "We talk about the Sipapu [place of Hopi emergence] as being a place of being always in our memories, our thoughts. It is only one of thousands of places like that. There are hundreds of shrines all over northern Arizona, and southern Utah, and southern Colorado that are connected in our minds and our consciousness. . . . We think of them in terms of 'what do they mean to us as a tribal people?' We know that this clan, that clan was there. We know that this is the place where you go to get a particular mineral, an herb, a particular plant. We are familiar that something happened there a long time ago that affected us. . . . It has an emotional content to it. We are emotionally connected to it, and that is why Hopis are emotionally connected to our landscape in its entirety. We can articulate that connection to hundreds, if not thousands of points on the landscape. So it is like a spider web that is connected to all of these things. And the Hopis are connected to the spider web. So we are all interconnected. And we cover this ground up here in our consciousness, in our subconscious, in our culture, in our language."

———

NO ONE REALLY knows when the Athabascan people first migrated into the North American Southwest. Estimates range from hundreds to thousands of years. Athabascan groups live in the far north of North America and may well precede Eskimo presence. In the Southwest, Athabascan lineage is reflected in Navajo and various Apache cultures. Until the nineteenth century, the Apaches and Navajos were hunter-gatherers. They vigorously fought off invading interlopers from the east who were intent in clearing the landscape of "hostile Indians" to make way for the entrepreneurs who justified their own existence by virtue of Manifest Destiny that guaranteed the right of westward expansion through "Divine Providence."

Joe Saenz is descended from the Warm Springs band of Chííhénee' or "Red Paint People" of Chiricahua Apaches who spawned Victorio, one of the most brilliant of the Apache guerilla warriors in the nineteenth century. Joe Saenz is a guide and outfitter who leads small groups into the Gila Wilderness and conveys Apache wisdom of his people.

"You know, one of the guiding terms that I like to keep in mind is that there's a time and a place for everything. I can't talk against money in the sense of what its value is because Apaches value trading. Apaches value economic interaction between groups. It was just as money, it was just as trade goods. But the motivation and the foundation of that trade was very different from what it is now. So I don't want to just talk against trading and the value of economics, but certainly what is traded and how it's traded is the big difference.

"To actively use an area and destroy its essence and destroy its foundation, that we don't believe in. That is where it becomes a problem. We harvest things on a renewable resource basis. In Apache culture, we preserve things and we kept things from just depleting and by not running them into the ground. Commerce and economics and the value of trade is very important there. But it was seen from a very different perspective. We didn't go in there and destroy an area to make money and then move on, like we'd never see it again or use it. That was just against what we understood and knew.

"And so the whole act of mining is very difficult to understand because of that. It's a difference of ideology, it's a difference of perspective. The differences are so profound that it led to war. It led to battle. It led to killing. But again, value, economics, trading, and money things, they have their place. But unfortunately, there's people that pass that boundary of reasonable renewable resource preservation and ideology of it.

"As far as our place, our being where we're supposed to exist—the place that we see ourselves is that we don't consider ourselves above Nature. We consider ourselves as a part of it. And so whatever we did to the environment, we did to ourselves. So the code of ethics for Apaches was peace and harmony—peace among people and harmony with the environment. And that pretty much set a standard that we had to live by. Whatever we did, we had to do in mind that we were not the only ones that were going to use it—that there were going to be generations behind us using it. There were going to be families behind us using it. There was going to be somebody right behind us using it afterwards.

"So the culture itself dictated our behavior in the environment. We had everything from what a lot of people consider as quaint mythology, mythological stories, stories of creation. But those stories were a distinctive outlay of our expected behavior. Everything from what animals you could eat, what animals you couldn't eat, when you could do certain functions or events, the structure of the family—all of that had stories that evolved and made a person understand the meaning of it. But if you take it a step further, you can see that they were also stories that were intended to provide a lesson of the environment. Taboo foods. In that period of time before settlement and before the American culture expanded to this country, we were basically supposed to eat four-legged, air-breathing, herd animals—not predators, nothing of that nature that controlled other herd animals. So that in itself was just a matter of culling the herd. Predators live alone, some of the predators hunt in small groups, stuff like that. We only ate animals that existed in large groups so they were easy to be replaced.

"Fish is a good example. Traditional Apaches did not eat fish. I lived in Alaska, and so I understood the value of the fish up there and how much fish it takes to keep a people fed. So I can see in this country traditionally, Gila trout was the only fish here. So through some mechanism, through some teaching, fish became a taboo food for us. I can see why. We would have decimated that population if we tried to eat that fish. There's just not enough fish here. So that in itself preserved the water, preserved the ecology of those animals and that existence there.

"Number of family—we understand that traditionally Apaches usually only had one child every four years. And that made sense because of the resources, the movement, practicality, defense, all of that. And so we have stories that acquaint us with evolution of culture of Apaches. I guess because of my upbringing and schooling and formal education and trying to look more at a scientific application to it, I can easily see why those were very strong and practical and very effective methods of teaching the people and passing that on to them.

"Apache culture was in many ways a holistic culture. It took in everything. And what we didn't have that we needed to use we learned very quickly, and sometimes we learned it extremely well. And that meant from hunting to existence in the environment to foods to everything that we had to adapt to or take advantage of or use the resource that was there. I think that everything, even music, song, the language, everything, had an integral part in how it formed that culture to allow us to exist like we did back then, again keeping to those codes of ethics, peace and harmony."

———

THE COLORADO PLATEAU is an enormous landform that rises in the very heart of the North American Southwest. It is red rock country bounded to the east by the Río Grande, to the west by the Río Colorado, to the north by the San Juan River, to the south, the Little Colorado. It is arid, desert-like. Yet it sustains the largest population of Indigenous people in the United States—the Navajo people. Their traditional culture was all but extirpated in the mid-nineteenth century when soldiers of Manifest Destiny captured thousands of Navajos and herded them hundreds of miles to the east to Bosque Redondo in a moment of infamy known to them as "the long walk." There they were held hostage for four years before being released to return to their beloved homeland of Dinetah throughout the Colorado Plateau. At that point, their population was estimated at between eight thousand and ten thousand. Today, they number nearly four hundred thousand, although many Navajos live off reservation.

Many years ago, I was fortunate to meet a Navajo man of rare consciousness and talent. His name is Roy Kady, and he lives near the base of the Carrizo Mountains where he tends to his flock of Churro sheep, and weaves truly fine pieces of fabric art that are highly prized. He is also a learned lore-master. One day, we climbed into his truck, and he drove us north along a formidable two-track to a bluff overlooking the San Juan River. There was an old traditional female hogan where Roy had been born. He invited me inside and I set up my recording equipment. Roy then lit his ceremonial pipe and blew the smoke over my recording equipment, over me, over himself, and throughout the hogan in a prayer of blessing. For the next while, he recounted for me part of the Navajo relationship to homeland by recounting his knowledge of the four sacred mountains.

Roy Kady:

"To the east we have Tsisnaasjini', and when you say the mountains and your offerings early morning, when you say, 'Tsisnaasjini', you're saying, 'In beauty may you surround me with a protection of a rainbow belt to protect me on my track, my daily track or in life.' When you say, 'Tsoodzil,' which is the south mountain, Mount Taylor, you're saying, 'Also give me the beautiful language of turquoise to give me the ability to communicate what I have to communicate today. May my words be all beautiful.; And then you say, 'Tsoodzil,' which is Mount Taylor. And then our west mountain is Dook'o'oosliid, and when you say, 'Dook'o'oosliid,' you say, 'From the tip of the peak of San Francisco, may you always have this beam of light to light where I'm going, whether it be day or night. May that beam always be bright for me so that I know my path, where I'm headed.' And then when you say, 'Dibe Nitsaa,' which is the northern mountain, Mount Hesperus, you're talking about the sacred sheep that we all know is the backbone of the Navajo society. That is a very sacred animal and that's why our fourth sacred mountain is named Dibe Nitsaa. With that we're strong, and the reason why sheep is so important—in a lot of our traditional stories that are told with all the monsters, it was the sheep, the bighorn sheep, that was the sole survivor of all poverty. Everything that has to do with poverty, the bighorn sheep withstood every test, even with the lightning gods. They've tried to strike him down, to cease him. But the bighorn sheep always survived and was the only animal to do that. And that's why the northern mountain stands for that mountain. It's the mountain that gives us strength. It's the mountain that is our protecting mountain. It has a lot of strength, and then that's why it's called Bighorn Sheep Mountain."

IMAGINE THE EARTH as the poly-bio-form that it is, urging evolution within its biotic plasma, birthing millions and millions of wildly diverse species over billions of years, seemingly edging into the evermore complex, spawning at least one species (and probably others) with the gift of refined consciousness. Consider our own species as but an individual example of a life-form at home in this robust yet fragile planetary community of life that characterizes that brief epoch we have characteristically dubbed "Anthropocene." In our anthropocentrism, many of us have gradually transitioned our focus away from tie to homeland as we quest for power, knowledge, wealth, and comfort—our pursuit of happiness—resulting in part in a virtualization of reality wherein our intuitions of kinship with our fellow species tend to atrophy.

Others of us have remained more in contact with homeland, have retained cultural systems of mores and attitudes that are commensurate with spirit of place, and thus are more intuitively in tune with the flow of Nature. No Indigenous human culture in direct contact with dominant monoculture is exempt from having been at least partially subsumed. It is my fervent hope that that same contact with traditional Indigenous peoples may conversely reveal to those rooted in monoculture that cultural diversity reflects bioregional diversity which itself reveals the complexity of the mosaic of geo-biotic communities that comprise our Earthly ecosystem. Cultural evolution occurs far more rapidly than biological evolution. If we as a species are to continue to evolve, our cultural evolution must surely include deep intuition of our kinship with all life. That lies at the heart of bioregional perspective, and it is that deep intuition of kinship that is part of the enormous contribution of our so-called Native American cultures, our Indigenous cultures that whisper their wisdom into the wind.

4. | Aldo Leopold in the Southwest

This essay originally appeared in El Palacio *(Fall 2009).*

"HE, OF ALL THE environmental thinkers I've read, put together perhaps the most cohesive view of the natural world, and he did it in a way that is more accessible and more persuasive than anyone else has done. So I see him as the essential man, the touchstone to whom we all go back, no matter our disagreements with him. And we should always be in tension with our mentors in a sense. We should always be re-examining what has been passed down to us.

"But he is a giant, and no one has given us a more complete view and a better expressed view than Aldo Leopold." So says author and environmentalist William de Buys, himself in the vanguard of a cadre of conservation-minded activists.

Indeed, Aldo Leopold was a giant whose influence continues to spread like a blaze fanned by the wind. He was born in Burlington, Iowa, in 1887, and died of a heart attack in 1948 while fighting a grassfire. The singed pages of an ever-present journal were found in his pocket.

Leopold grew up in a house that overlooked the Mississippi River. He attended the Yale School of Forestry, graduated with a master's degree in 1909, and at that point a century ago, made a move that would change his life and his mind: Aldo Leopold came to the North American Southwest. It was here that his thinking was refined by the rough and tumble reality of this arid landscape then sparsely populated by Indians, Hispanos, and ranchers, all of whom took their survival cues from the flow of Nature.

In those days, many recalled the Indian wars that had dominated the nineteenth century. Those ranchers and rangers who rode the rangeland considered shooting bear, bobcats, cougars, and wolves to be their contribution to taming the West. Young Aldo was no exception. There are photos of him astride his horse, the very image of the pistol-packin' hero of cowpoke mythology.

His first job was in the Apache National Forest in the Arizona Territory where he became deeply attached to the landscape. In 1911, he was transferred to the Carson National Forest in northern New Mexico where he achieved his great ambition to become the supervisor of a national forest. It was during this period that he met Estella Luna Bergere, a lady born into one of New Mexico's oldest and most distinguished families. They fell in love and were married in 1912. Together, they built their first home, a rustic hand-hewn cabin situated in Tres Piedras, New Mexico. It was from here that the new supervisor administered the Carson National Forest.

Leopold spent much of his working life on horseback. The Carson National Forest is spread across different ranger districts that span an immense landscape. At one point he was returning from a trip to Durango, and while riding through the Jicarilla Ranger District, harsh weather knocked him right out of the saddle.

His younger daughter, Estella, now eighty-three (in 2009) and Professor Emerita, Department of Biology at the University of Washington, Seattle, recounts that her father "was sick for two years flat after he had ridden across a pass and a snowstorm fell on him. Everything was wet, and he had to sleep in that wet bedroll for a couple of nights. By the time he made it to Mother, to home, he had a bad kidney infection, or condition, and it knocked him out for a couple of years. It was terrible."

Once he was well enough to work again, Leopold took a position as the executive secretary for the Albuquerque Chamber of Commerce. During this period, he befriended a young insurance executive and fellow midwesterner, and the ramifications of his friendship with Clinton B. Anderson had extraordinary significance. As Stewart Udall recalled in a speech given at the Sixth National Wilderness Conference in Santa Fe in 1994, "Anderson developed a love affair with the natural world. He acquired many of his conservation convictions as a result of a friendship he formed with Aldo Leopold . . . on trips they made into nearby mountains."

Leopold returned to the US Forest Service after World War I and was assigned the position of assistant regional forester in charge of operations throughout some twenty million acres within the Southwest. He revisited areas he had first seen ten years earlier and was deeply aware of how the lands had eroded.

Courtney White is the author of *Revolution on the Range*, and cofounder and former executive director of the Quivira Coalition in Santa Fe, an organization dedicated to "broadcasting the principles of ecologically sensitive ranch management." He explains,

"Leopold saw tremendous gullying, deep arroyos in these landscapes that he suspected were not natural as he was taught. He began to make connections between grass and soil and rain and slope and overgrazing, principally by cattle. He wasn't anti-grazing but he certainly was anti-bad management. Leopold wrote an amazing essay called 'Pioneers and Gullies' published in *Sunset* magazine of all places—one of the popular magazines—in 1924, where he decries the pioneer attitude towards land and how they just had come in, taken a European way of living in a wetter environment with certain kinds of agricultural practices, put it in an environment that he called a 'hair-trigger ecological environment,' meaning the desert Southwest—and not understood the effects."

Leopold scholar Susan Flader, board member of the Aldo Leopold Foundation in Baraboo, Wisconsin, advanced the notion that this concept became the basis for his celebrated essay, "The Land Ethic," that appears as the final piece in Leopold's masterwork, *A Sand County Almanac*.

It was apparently in the Jicarilla Ranger District of the Carson National Forest where Leopold seriously ruminated on cattle-wrought erosion, the same ranger district where earlier he was stricken with the near fatal kidney malaise. It was at the north end of this ranger district that I served as a fire lookout atop Caracas Mesa for three seasons during the 1960s. Few cattle ranged there during my time, but evidence of the presence of cattle, sheep and horses remained. It was through this same forest that the Old Spanish Trail had meandered during the Mexican Period of the nineteenth century when caravans of traders wended west to California where sheep were sold, and New Mexican trade goods were swapped for horses that were driven back to New Mexico. A herd of wild horses still ranged throughout the Jicarilla landscape.

Camped beneath that open sky for months at a time, looking out over a vast landscape, listening to the wind pass through the Ponderosa Pines, hearing occasional choruses of wild turkeys and coyotes, visiting with deer and bobcats, watching eagles hover, and savoring the night time when no light of human provenance intruded, I came to know my own kinship with the wild, to recognize that an ethical relationship to homeland comes from within, and that Aldo Leopold had hit the mark as he clearly articulated his own deep wisdom that was to influence generations as yet unborn.

Susan Flader reveals,

"There is a concept that he got from Ouspensky (Russian philosopher and author of *Tertium Organum*), although he never credits Ouspensky directly with it. It's the concept of the noumenon as distinct from phenomenon: phenomenon being the outward manifestation which you can easily see and understand, and the noumenon being the inner meaning, the essence of something. One of the first times that he wrote about it was actually in another unpublished manuscript. He was writing a book on Southwestern game fields. In one of the early chapters, he writes about the deer as the noumenon of the Southwestern mountains. He says, 'Without the presence of the deer or the possibility of seeing a deer in each new dip and bend in the hillside, the Southwest would be empty, a spiritual vacuum.'"

Leopold perceived deer as the noumenon of the wild Southwest. Later he would regard the wolf, which he and others had caused to be extirpated from the landscape, to be the noumenon of the wild. He would laud every attempt to restore the wolf to the Southwest, so that the green fire of the wolf's eyes could burn once again in the mind of the mountain. The presence of the noumenon embellished Leopold's vision of the Spirit of Nature.

William de Buys expands this notion when he says, "One of the things that I think he glimpsed that is now sort of a cornerstone of ecological thinking is the idea of energy flowing through land: of water moving, of air moving, of nutrients moving and so forth. He had this vision, this integrated holistic vision, of the flows through the ecosystem, and they took place often within the watershed unit. So he saw the watershed as being a primary unit for land management and even more for land understanding."

Nina Leopold Bradley remarked on the breadth of her father's scope: "I could say that he is the most religious person I ever knew, and he never went inside of a church. He knew right from wrong. He lived his life ethically. He, I guess, didn't need the guidance of a deity. . . . He was always teaching us, but never did you know he was teaching us. If you asked him a question, then he would just do everything to try to draw you out, make you think. But he never said, 'This is so-and-so, and you should understand that it is related to the things next to it.' He was very subtle in the way he taught."

In 1922, Aldo Leopold submitted a formal proposal that part of the Gila National Forest of southern New Mexico be administrated as a wilderness area off limits to vehicular traffic, mining, timbering, and heavy machinery. His proposal was accepted by the Forest Service in 1924, and thus the Gila Wilderness became the first such wilderness area in the United States. Forty years later, the Wilderness Act was passed into federal law. The passage of this occurred on the watch of Stewart Udall during his tenure as Secretary of the Interior.

In the words of Stewart Udall,

"Clinton Anderson was an insurance man in Albuquerque, and he and Leopold became friends. I think this is probably in the early 1920s in Albuquerque. They used to discuss the national forests, and

Leopold convinced Anderson that the Wilderness Bill was a good idea and there should be a law protecting wilderness. Anderson became a congressman and . . . became a senator in 1948 and he became chairman of the Interior and Insular Affairs Committee in 1960 right after Kennedy was elected. He went to the White House, and he told Kennedy to sponsor a wilderness bill, and he handed him a copy of his bill, Senate Bill 5. He said, 'Call for the enactment of a wilderness bill.' Kennedy agreed and put it in his conservation message . . . Lyndon Johnson signed it [Wilderness Bill] into law, I think in September 1964."

Thus the trail was blazed for protecting wilderness for its own sake.

Aldo Leopold twice journeyed into the Río Gavilan watershed in northwestern Mexico. It was here that he stepped into what he regarded as true, unsullied wilderness for the first time. He perceived that earlier on, people had lived in this watershed and had fashioned terraces and check dams where small plots of land had once been transformed into gardens and were now long abandoned to the deer and other wild creatures. Leopold wrote his provocative essay entitled "Song of the Gavilan" wherein he reflected on how indeed humans had lived in harmony with this habitat. His essay clearly reveals the nature of his mind and intuitions: "On a still night, when the campfire is low and the Pleiades have climbed over rimrocks, sit quietly and listen for a wolf to howl, and think hard of everything you have seen and tried to understand. Then you may hear it—a vast pulsing harmony—its score inscribed on a thousand hills, its notes the lives and deaths of plants and animals, its rhythms spanning the seconds and centuries."

Gary Paul Nabhan is the author of many books and is regarded as one of America's great natural historians: "You know, I've been meditating on Aldo Leopold's second trip in the Río Gavilán in the Chihuahuan borderlands that he took with his brother Carl and his son Starker and a number of friends from both New Mexico and Chihuahua. It was ostensibly a hunting trip, but what he harvested there was far more than venison or quail or bear meat. What he found there was the concept of ecosystem health that we now use. He called it ecological health. That concept included rather than excluded land-based cultures. And after living in New Mexico with the Luna family, after growing up in Iowa among many land-based ethnic cultures, he had this in his background (the understanding) that stewardship of the land, whether it's done by hunters and gatherers or whether it's done by farmers and ranchers, can stabilize, enhance, or restore the diversity of depleted places and does not inextricably mean that humans will deplete that diversity."

In 1944, Aldo Leopold wrote an essay titled "Thinking Like a Mountain" wherein he reflected on an incident that had occurred in 1909 when he was still a greenhorn ranger in the Blue Range of the Arizona Territory. He and others happened onto a small pack of wolves. They emptied their rifles into the wolf pack, and as they examined the carnage, one wolf still lived. Leopold looked into the eyes of this dying wolf and watched the wild, green fire in those eyes blink out. The memory haunted him into an epiphany of recognition that the living spirit of the wolf was integral to the mind of the mountain. It took thirty-five years for this epiphany to be fully realized and manifested in one of his greatest essays that appears in *A Sand County Almanac*.

Sand County is located in Wisconsin where Aldo Leopold, his wife Estella, his sons Starker, Carl and Luna, and his daughters Nina and Estella lived for many years. It was here that Leopold purchased a soil-starved farm, rebuilt the Shack into a livable dwelling, and over the weekends of the rest of his life restored the wasted land to wildness. The Leopold family were tightly knit. They worked together to restore the land, and they played together and ate together. Aldo and his wife, Estella sat at the dinner table and held hands throughout their marriage. Their daughter, also named Estella had this to say: "Mom was wonderful. And they were very, very close. Dad came home every noon for lunch and walked in the door and Mother would greet him with her apron on and they would hug, and he would say, 'Estella, the house looks so beautiful. How do you do it?' and sit down and have lunch and hold hands, which was great. They were very warm, and she was, of course, very supportive."

Nina Leopold Bradley recalls, "Dad had a wonderful sense of humor. There was never any small talk around Dad. It was always very, very serious. But if something really captured him, he would just dissolve. I remember one time my sister (Estella) was late in arriving at the shack. We were all there for the weekend. So she took the train and her bicycle and her pet—her pet squirrel—and took the train to Baraboo and then rode her bike in to the edge of the marsh, and then she had to swim across the marsh. My father and I, we just happened to be out taking a walk and Dad saw this creature swimming along with this squirrel on her head, and I thought he was going to collapse in laughter. He just absolutely broke down. He had a wonderful sense of humor."

The entire Leopold family brought their land in Sand County back into a state of wild balance and harmony, actually practicing restoration ecology, the concept for which had germinated in Leopold's mind during his years in the Southwest as he gazed out over cattle-burnt lands. He wrote *A Sand County Almanac* in Wisconsin from within the fomentation of a mind honed in the Southwest, a mind that came to understand independently what John Wesley Powell had realized half a century earlier, that the watershed is the basic component within the mosaic of watersheds in the arid landscape of the American West.

As scholar Susan Flader points out, "He (Leopold) was invited to give the John Wesley Powell address to the Southwestern Division of the American Association of Science. He took as his title, 'The Conservation Ethic.' That was the first published version of what would later, after several other principal addresses over the years, be combined in his seminal article, 'The Land Ethic,' which is the capstone of *A Sand County Almanac*. ... It has seemed to me that his concept of the land ethic grew very much out of his concern for the southwestern watersheds and the problem of soil erosion."

For generations, America and Western culture have been

dominated by an economic paradigm founded largely on turning habitat into money. Aldo Leopold came to understand the folly and error of that thinking over sixty years ago. He also came to understand that we as a species are but a single species within the community of life on our planet, and that indeed we are rooted in Nature. At this point in time, it is absolutely imperative that we heed the heart of his message in this final essay from *A Sand County Almanac*:

"A land ethic, then, reflects the existence of an ecological conscience, and this in turn reflects a conviction of individual responsibility for the health of the land. Health is the capacity of the land for self-renewal. Conservation is our effort to understand and preserve this capacity . . . Quit thinking about land-use as solely an economic problem. Examine each question in terms of what is ethically and esthetically right, as well as what is economically expedient. A thing is right when it tends to preserve the integrity, stability, and beauty of the biotic community. It is wrong when it tends otherwise. . . . By and large our present problem is one of attitudes."

5. | Averting Dystopia

This essay originally appears in Green Fire Times *(January 2016).*

ARID NEW MEXICO, WHERE distant mountain ranges mark far horizons that encompass vast living emptiness, where major ecosystems are easily distinguished one from the other, where waterways are modest in their yield and thus recognized and valued as the life-giving source, where the sky is an upturned bowl of blue wherein clouds dance over mountains and refine human imagination, where wind passes through the grasses and rustles the boughs of mountain pines, where the greater chorus of the biotic community sings praise to existence—this is homeland so powerful as to grab the undivided attention of those with the consciousness to perceive meaning beyond personal self.

There are appropriate ways to live within, to participate in such a landscape. A prime pre-requisite is to develop an abiding mindfulness of the needs of the landscape, which is itself, a mosaic of habitats, of biotic communities, of ecosystems, of watersheds integrated into a pattern whose complexity requires a lifetime of applied intelligence and intuition to even partially understand.

We humans have proven ourselves a peripatetic lot, constantly on the move though most of us have long since abandoned hunting and gathering as a lifeway. Here in New Mexico, there remain cultures that are still rooted to landscape. There are Indian pueblos that have long adorned the banks of the northern Río Grande. There are Hispano communities sustained by the land, umbilicated to the *río* and *ritos* by acequias. And while no community is exempt from the economic imperative imposed on everyone by the dominant human culture, there remain Indigenous cultural recollections within native communities that are treasure troves of both practice and attitude that are vital to home habitat.

There is also an extraordinary scientific culture of practice in New Mexico that includes two national laboratories, a thriving university system, a spectacular radio telescope, and myriad scientific waystations scattered throughout. And there is a burgeoning back-to-the-flow-of-Nature culture of practice that had its genesis in the counterculture movement when this land of clear light beckoned thousands of youth disillusioned with the consumer-driven post-WWII American Dream.

This landscape has been as a magnet for adventurous humans for at least 12,000 years. Fairly recently, it has come to be called New Mexico, and in the 121,000 square miles of surface area presently contained within its geopolitical boundaries, there is less surface water relative to size than in any other state. Aridity is the prevailing characteristic. Governance has long been associated with water availability.

The acequia systems put in place by Hispano communities are based on equitably sharing the water during both wet and dry years. Ancestral Puebloans were ostensibly driven from their homelands in and around Chaco Canyon when a major drought hit nearly a thousand years ago causing many of their descendants to resettle along the Río Grande, a more permanent body of running water. Traditional Pueblo Indians perceive natural landscape as a great commons to be shared by all living creatures. The eminent human ecologist, Garrett Hardin pointed out that the commons works as long as the human population does not grow too great. At which point the commons must be governed. Success is determined by who governs and how well. Elinor Ostrom pointed out that nowhere in his essay, "The Tragedy of the Commons," does Hardin include such words as "trust" or "mutual cooperation."

Governance itself becomes an enormous problem. It may begin as an ideal as with the United States two and a half centuries ago when democracy was clearly defined and put into practice. But over time, human political hierarchy in consonance with individual and finally corporate quest for riches has endangered the commons, has jeopardized habitat. This is especially true when the human population, with its inequitable scale of standards of living, has finally exceeded the carrying capacity of the planetary commons. Referring to corporate control of government, Ed Abbey aptly said, "A patriot must always be ready to defend his country against his government." The human population of the planet has grown by well over a billion souls since Ed died thirty-three years ago (as of 2022), and the disparity between the rich and the poor has increased exponentially as vast habitat has been pillaged inexorably. All the while, the Internet has become an enormous factor in preservation and dispersal within the commons of human consciousness.

And so how do we imagine our future in New Mexico? Some years ago, farmer/author Wendell Berry adamantly reminded me that he wasn't into predicting the future, citing Christ's aphorism, "Sufficient unto the day is the evil thereof." I agree that we cannot predict the future, but with sufficient collective energy, we can nudge at least one force of Nature in the direction of relative balance. It was our great friend Rina Swentzell who vigorously reminded me that the human species has become just such a force. Indeed, we as a species have become such a force of Nature, such a dominant manipulative species, that we are deeply affecting the flow of Nature on this planet Earth that gave birth to us some ten thousand or so generations ago.

———

IT WAS NEARLY half-century ago at a meeting of the Santa Fe County Commission that then chairman Art Trujillo advised those of us living in Santa Fe Canyon to form a neighborhood association to give grassroots voice in defense of our future. We did, and we elected Willie Apodaca as our president, and Pat Feather as our secretary/treasurer. We canvassed the entire neighborhood to gather perspective. Virtually everyone agreed that we wanted to keep Cerro Gordo Park as a natural area rather than have it become a paved over tennis court surrounded by high wire fencing complete with nightlights that would despoil the character of the canyon, as defined in the proposal as forwarded by then Mayor Louie Montaño. We prepared a petition that was signed by almost everyone in the neighborhood.

The evening arrived when Louie's proposal was put to test by the Santa Fe City Council. Mayor Montaño who was presiding, had prepared his own petition with many signatures that attested that the park should be turned into Louie's nightmare of progress. When input from the audience was requested by himself, my old friend and neighbor Gregorita Rodriguez, a renowned *curandera* and woman of wisdom, asked me to help her up to the podium. I held her elbow as she spoke into the microphone for all to hear. She said, "Louie, that petition you got there was signed by people who been dead for over ten years!" Louie slumped in his chair as the audience cheered, and we won the right to keep the park natural by a single vote.

Today, politics is regarded with cynicism by almost everyone including many politicians dominated by their corporate regime. We in New Mexico have two fine honest men who serve as senators in the Congress of the United States. Tom Udall (now retired) and Martin Heinrich are both deeply rooted in environmental ethics. I personally know this to be so.

Not long after our victory over Cerro Gordo Park, I called Tom's father, Stewart Udall, and asked him what advice he would proffer to Santa Fe as we edge into an uncertain future. Stewart's primary advice was that we should create a green belt surrounding the city where we could grow and graze food to thus become as self-sufficient as we could. Stewart had grown up on a farm in St. Johns, Arizona, during the Great Depression, and well knew the importance of self-sufficiency. This lifestyle had shaped much of his thinking during his tenure as Secretary of the Interior throughout the Kennedy and Johnson administrations.

I've been extremely fortunate in my own long life to have met and befriended many whose opinions I value and whose perspectives have long contributed to my own. For well over half a century I've been involved in one way or another in the environmental movement. I continue to work every day in behalf of what I interpret as the greatest good that includes seeking to comprehend the relationship between biological and cultural diversity within the great mosaic of geophysical regions that comprise the spherical face of our planet.

My great hope is that we learn to live sustainably within our respective homeland, our home watershed with as full and complete an understanding of the needs of homeland as we can muster, and that those needs supersede our own presumed needs if indeed we are to be sustained therein. This includes a large measure of grassroots governance from within the commons based on mutual cooperation and trust. At any meeting of any governing body, home habitat must sit metaphorically at the head of the table. We are equipped to intuit and recognize what is ethically correct and thus proceed accordingly.

I envision a tremendous shift of cultural attitude away from the prevailing economically dominated paradigm to an ecologically sound system of principles. I recognize the need for partial decentralization from governance on high—governance now held in sway by the corporate-industrial-military complex that we were warned away from by President Eisenhower just before he left office in 1961. I envision some form of "polycentric governance" as presented by Elinor Ostrom in her fine book, *Governing the Commons*, for which she received the Nobel Prize in 2009. This occurs within different levels of governance extending from the halls of Congress to the grassroots where the real action is, where the knowledge base is, where people actually abide in their home habitats, their home eco-regions.

From this mode of envisioning, I recommend three books. The first is *Desert Solitaire* by Edward Abbey that can fire up one's personal sense of conviction. The second is *The Practice of the Wild* by Gary Snyder that provides deep insight into a state of mind to which we must aspire to become rooted in homeland. The third is *Thinking Like a Watershed*, an anthology of papers and transcribed interviews with leading thinkers from within Indigenous communities and more recent cultures of practice that present alternative perspectives, edited by Jack and Celestia Loeffler.

To reiterate what my great friend Rina Swentzell pointed out, the human species has become a force of Nature. What a travesty if we as a species fail to muster the consciousness to recognize that our planet is our homeland, not a place to be shunned or plundered, but rather revered, honored, and loved—and restored.

Thus, we proceed in beauty.

6. | LUCA's Dream

This essay originally appeared in Green Fire Times *(December 2012).*

THE EARTH HAS CIRCLED around the Sun over 3.5 billion times since that special microbe evolved within the primordial milieu that characterized our planet some ten billion or so solar years after our universe blasted into being. This tiny dot of RNA was equipped with a genome. It could replicate itself. It was alive. It was LUCA, ostensibly the last universal common ancestor of all life that has spanned time on our now living planet Earth. Thus, it is likely that we, as the human species retain elements of the genetic code that resided in LUCA.

Metaphorically, LUCA was the seed of life that gradually blossomed into billions of species, and lately—relative to geologic time—consciousness. LUCA spawned Life and Consciousness, a complex dimension through which the universe may be perceived, contemplated, and partly understood, perhaps a window through which our universe may perceive itself.

We are the recipients of LUCA's potential. We, and the rest of life on Earth are the cast of LUCA's dream. Long may it last.

In the biblical Book of Genesis, creation lasted seven days. It took us a week to get from nothingness to here. Referring to the great Tome of Science, if we symbolically conceive of 500 million years as a day, it took six days for LUCA's dream to span the planet with small unicellular organisms—and on the seventh day, the Cambrian Explosion burst upon the planet marking the dawn of the Paleozoic Era when multicellular life forms gradually fomented over time into ever more complex organisms, thwarted occasionally by great spasms of extinction, diversity of life always recovering, always changing. Humanity blinked into being achieving species-hood only two or three hundred thousand years ago.

Evolution, as interpreted by Charles Darwin and his intellectual descendants, provides a conscious reflection on LUCA's evolving dream that presently results in recognition of the miracle that exists in our tiny space in the universe. If life and consciousness prevail here on our planet Earth, considering that our Sun is but one of two hundred billion or more stars in our Milky Way galaxy, and that the Milky Way is but one of possibly two hundred billion or more galaxies in the universe, human imagination still has a very long way to go to grasp the potential that exists in the universe. And in the great "Tome of Science," new pages are being written about the possibility of other concurrently happening universes, perhaps infinite in number.

This is our glimpse into the Great Mystery available to be pondered at any moment as long as we live, and as long as we survive as a species . . .

Now is not the time to squander our ponderings by focusing on so much that is irrelevant relative to our continued existence.

Our species is currently engaged in a time of hastening cultural evolution that far outstrips biological evolution. Our collective consciousness is presently offering an extraordinary palette of potential areas of focus. Our species is fragmented into highly diverse cultural systems of practice, themselves having blossomed, withered, and remanifested myriad times over the last twelve thousand or so years since the final days of last Ice Age. Then we existed in bands of hunter-gatherers and were concerned that we owned no more than we could carry. Our scale of cultural perspective had yet to expand beyond subsistence necessary for survival. Evidence strongly suggests that we were egalitarians, that social hierarchy was thwarted by the need to practice mutual cooperation within the band and beyond, that tyrannical bullies were kept in check by the advent of weapons that could strike from afar.

With the coming of the warming trends of the Holocene, so came the advent of agriculture. We gradually became more sedentary and settled into villages, towns, and eventually cities, less inclined to the nomadic ways of our forbearers, more inclined to pursue accumulating wealth. Some were more successful at this than others, thus social hierarchy became an organizing factor in human culture. Perhaps this is in keeping with humanity's place in the animal kingdom. Civilizations appeared autonomously around the world. Curiously, evidence reveals that many civilizations waned during periods of extended drought—something to bear in mind as we challenge the elements.

Concurrently, spiritual realms crystallized into religions. Many of the gods were taken out of Nature and relocated in heavenly or hellish realms available to human souls only after death. Gradually, much of the landscape was secularized. Human sense of kinship with the rest of life began and continues to wane. Thus we perceive ourselves as separate from LUCA's dream, imagining ourselves to be Nature's reason-to-be in this age we have dubbed the Anthropocene. Indeed, we are presently the dominant species . . . but for how long?

That we as a species have achieved such an evolved level of consciousness is awe-inspiring. No one knows of other planets that are alive let alone spawning life-forms capable of consciousness. Surely we are not alone in the universe, or even our home galaxy.

Certain pages in the Tome of Science reveal that it is possible that billions of solar years hence, the universe will rip apart perhaps to reassemble in a new incarnation. Before then, our Sun will have expanded in size, "obliviating" our planet Earth. Other pages reveal possible perspectives that we are but holograms dancing to the delight of elsewhere imaginations. Or that there are parallel universes mirroring our own. Or that the notion that our universe, though appearing infinite is rather but one of an infinite number of universes.

The truth is, we are here and now. That tiny dot of life known as LUCA of billennia past has resulted thus far in a level of complexity of life and consciousness and attendant technology and collective lifestyle that we as a species now strain the capacity of our planet to sustain. The last three centuries have been witness to a great rise in human population and industry, extraction and expenditure of nonrenewable resources, energy consumption, pollution, scientific data, lengthening human lifespan, tempering infant mortality, medical arts, education, standard of living capability, sophistication of media, and now digital technology. The Industrial Revolution set the stage for the twentieth century wherein our human population more than tripled as did human appetite and consumption.

Today we are beginning to perceive the presence of climate change and climate instability. We face grave jeopardy because of our own carelessness and lack of timely response to warnings by James Hansen and other scientists who watch with dismay as CO_2 levels continue to rise in spite of their repeated warnings.

I personally think that the greatest single problem we must address is our systems of cultural attitudes. Until we recognize that our ecology is far more important than our economy, we will not arrest the juggernaut of our own invention. We must achieve something akin to a steady state economy and stay further population growth if we are to establish any kind of sustainable balance within our planetary ecosystem. We have allowed economics to become the dominant force that now drives our collective perspective. A certain amount of avarice has crept in—a nasty word for a nasty human characteristic that defines the Midas approach to ultimate disaster. The territorial imperative is now defined in national and other political boundaries that carve the commons into unnatural apportionments denying rather than welcoming recognition of kinship implied in LUCA's dream.

We are a crisis-driven species in a finite world. Our crises are more than plentiful, each tinged with a cultural bias. The keystone of our species-hood is showing points of stress and potential collapse. No matter where we look, there we are, each of us surviving as best we can, our spoor in our wake, none of us leaving a traceless passage through life and consciousness—especially in the virtual world of the Internet.

Consciousness is our greatest commons. It is filled with what we put into it: our thoughts, the words we utter, our writings, world and local news, documentary films, TV entertainments, arts and sciences,

Twitters, Skypes, Facebooks, cell phone calls, radio programs, musical compositions, our poetry, advertisements, spam—the shared perceptions of our senses, intellect, intuitions, and emotions. In our "march of progress," we have largely neglected the presence of Indigenous mind, offered by those of us who yet remain traditionally rooted to homeland, who continue to recognize kinship with all living creatures on our planet Earth that spawned LUCA 3.5 billion years ago.

We who reside in the landscape presently known as New Mexico live in a state of grace. Biodiversity and cultural diversity abound. Indigenous mind, scientific mind, artistic mind, musical mind, sustainable mind, and conscious mind circulate in overlapping cultures of practice that invigorate a level of cognitive diversity unique on our planet. Almost all of us can look beyond our windows into the exquisite habitat in which we share membership. Every creature, every plant is kindred. Each of us is part of the flow of Nature that sustains our planet Earth, our solar system, our galaxy, our universe from the microcosm to the macrocosm. That is the most significant concept that we can both digest and plant as a new seed so that we may grow to maturity from the grass roots and continue to evolve. We are part of LUCA's dream.

7. | Conflicting Ideologies

This essay originally appeared in Green Fire Times *(January 2017).*

WE, THE HUMAN SPECIES have been around for at least a couple hundred thousand years. For most of our species' 200,000-to-300,000-year timespan, we've lived as hunter-gatherers in relative balance with our biotic communities. But around 12,000 years ago, when the planet warmed up at the end of the last ice age, we humans began to practice agriculture, and thereafter collectively morphed into hierarchical societies that spread around the planet. Social hierarchy and economics became inextricably interlinked, and thus recent human cultures can be viewed through time as "haves and have nots," masters and slaves, privileged classes served by serfs, divinely anointed monarchs lording it over entire populations and their habitats.

At this point in the twenty-first century, the Divine Right of Kings has transmogrified into the corporate right of first refusal. Economics based on endless continuous growth empowers our cultural paradigm. Most of us are still serfs, although we have gained the right to vote, at least in nations that are ostensibly democracies. But in the main, it seems to me, most of those who run for public office dance to the endless drumbeat of a system of economics that so deafens them that they—and we—evade the profound reality that endless growth in a world of finite resources cannot be eternally sustained. Thus, ecological collapse is inevitable. As arch-conservative Ayn Rand pointed out, "We can evade reality, but we cannot evade the consequences of evading reality."

Over three decades ago, I recorded my friend Dave Foreman, a founder of Earth First! who had previously worked for many years with environmental organizations to save wilderness areas. He summed up his thinking as follows:

"I basically came to the conclusion that we were being co-opted by the establishment, that having influence and all made us moderate. We compromised more, thought about pragmatic politics instead of biocentric ethics. And so with several other people who had worked for the Friends of the Earth or the Wilderness Society, or who were active Sierra Club members, we decided that the time had come for an environmental group that wouldn't compromise, that would base itself on ethics rather than pragmatics, and that would take strong action to try to stop the destruction of wilderness. . . .

"If you look at the human race not as the consciousness of the Earth, but as the cancer of the Earth—that we're a disease ecologically—maybe Nature has evolved some of us as anti-bodies. That's the only way I can explain why some of us love wilderness and other people have no conception of it at all. And so, our role in the future, I think, is to try to preserve as many areas of natural diversity as possible. . . . And hopefully also develop the ethics and the potential for a human society that can live in harmony with the rest of the planet after this industrial madness burns itself out. Those are the two things I'm trying to do in the long term. One is to lay the groundwork for a human society in the future that is ecologically based, and the other is to preserve as much natural diversity now as we can."

Members of Earth First! were greatly inspired by Edward Abbey whose literary works include *Desert Solitaire* and *The Monkey Wrench Gang*, books that invigorated a subculture to react against turning habitat into money, that prevailing tenet of the corporate will.

On New Year's Day 1983, Ed and I returned from a camping trip in the Superstition Mountains to his writing cabin in the Sonoran Desert where I recorded him thinking out loud:

"I think by virtue of reason, common sense, the evidence of our good five bodily senses and daily experience, we can imagine a better way to live, with fairly simple solutions. Not easy—but simple.

Beginning here in America—we should set the example. We have set the example by pillaging the planet, and we should set the example for preserving life, including human life. First, most important, reduce human numbers, gradually, by normal attrition, letting the senile old farts like you and me die off. Reduce the human population to a reasonable number—for the United States something like 100 million, or even 50 million should be plenty. And then, second, simplify our needs and demands, so that we're not preying to excess on other forms of life—plant life and animal life—by developing new attitudes, a natural reverence for all forms of life."

These perspectives were voiced nearly forty years ago by a man who had become actively engaged in protecting homeland.

Early-twentieth-century America luxuriated in the fruits of the Industrial Revolution. But the stock market crash of 1929 was followed by the Great Depression that lasted till 1942 when the United States fully engaged in World War II that ended in 1945. Sixteen years of cultural "belt tightening" set Americans up to sanction unprecedented proliferation of consumerism. World leaders met in Bretton Woods, New Hampshire, in 1944, just before the end of the war to create an economic system that was to result in the World Bank and the global economy.

In 2013, I recorded yet another old friend, Jerry Mander, who wrote *The Capitalism Papers: Fatal Flaws of an Obsolete System*:

"Consumerism is what was going to save the economy. That was a conscious statement made during the 1950s post-Bretton Woods. Consumerism was going to be the answer. More and more products, more and more resources. There was not even the beginning of a thought about any limits to that potential. The environmental movement hadn't really even begun yet in any meaningful way. There were individuals like Edward Abbey and people like that who were talking in environmental terms, but there was no movement, there was no conscious sense of limits to any of that. And it was all about economic growth and individual consumption and getting ahead and competition and investment and advancement in the corporate world."

About that time, the counterculture happened. First hundreds then thousands of young Americans reacted against the consumer-based economy. Many moved into urban neighborhoods and "turned on, tuned in, and dropped out," following a new maxim voiced by Timothy Leary. Myriad experiments, both social and drug-induced, reshaped countercultural consciousness. Many were inspired to leave the cities and either live in newly founded communes or pursue life as individuals whose active imaginations far exceeded the parameters of the economic paradigm that dominated mainstream culture.

Gary Snyder emerged early on as a talented poet whose work was far more "naturistic" than urban-oriented, as were the works of his citified contemporaries Allen Ginsberg, Jack Kerouac, Gregory Corso, and others of the Beat generation. Gary was and remains a great voice in behalf of an ecologically motivated system of attitudes. In 1969, he wrote a piece of prose inspired by his understanding of Nature's flow, and the imminent jeopardy to earthly habitat. The piece is titled *Four Changes*, first published in 1970, and addresses four major issues: population, pollution, consumption, and transformation. It appears in various of Gary's books, including *Turtle Island*, for which he was awarded the Pulitzer Prize for poetry in 1975.

Between Snyder's *Four Changes* and Abbey's *Desert Solitaire*, a new bridge of perspective changed the face of social activism by introducing protection of the natural environment into the stream of countercultural consciousness in America. Thence environmental activism was born. Radical environmentalism became a factor as small groups or even cells of hardcore activists went to work.

Radical environmentalism is indeed hard work. It challenges the status quo to the limits. Scientists have provided the world public with a hard truth—namely that we've overloaded the atmosphere with carbon dioxide to the extent that our planet's climate must inevitably change resulting in growing risk to our species and many others, too many of which have already gone extinct as a result of human folly. Environmentalists are now pitted against the corporate/political/ military/industrial complex, itself dominated by leaders with apparently limited to zero understanding of the imminence of eco-disaster that is even now befalling our biotic community.

What's to be done?

The "grassroots" is the place to start with habitat-based expanding cadres deeply rooted and well-educated to the nature of respective watersheds and bioregions. Decentralization of political and corporate power is essential. We are governed by those whose unbridled economic and politically dark interests pose an existential threat to habitat. They must be thwarted through imagination, not force. This means invoking an enormous shift of attitude in mainstream culture.

The so-called millennial generation is the inheritor of what has gone before. This generation is savvy to digital media in a way heretofore unknown. Social media is a path to revolution using imagination and perseverance. A recent election was won by trumping the truth with deceit on many fronts. Social media can be used as a powerful force to reveal the truth and counter those forces that would bring us to ecological ruin. However, we must always retain recognition of our rootedness in the flow of Nature, while expanding intellectual and intuitive scope. We must invigorate a Nature-based gestalt of such magnitude that it overwhelms the current economic/political/cultural paradigm. We must induce a new cultural attitude based on compassion for our planet, this tiny watershed floating in space that spawned us and sustains us. We must run counter to the cultural continuum that threatens life as we know it.

That's a lot of expostulations in a row. But we are now engaged in a battle between conflicting ideologies, one of which is based on economic growth for its own sake that is strangling democracy and raping habitat, and the other founded in a system of ethics that honors life and consciousness within the biotic community that sustains us. This is not necessarily a contest between good and evil, but rather a collective choice between survival through moderation, or extinction through overindulgence in resources and power. To turn the juggernaut requires understanding exactly what is at stake and why, and thereafter becoming individually and collectively active. Intelligent civil disobedience will undoubtedly become a necessity. Reacting against legislation that violates natural order becomes imperative, first by clearly articulating the issues, and if that is insufficient, then through civil disobedience. Reciprocity with the biotic community is paramount and therefore must overturn legislation passed by politicians subject to corporate will. We are poignantly reminded of this as we regard our Indian brothers and sisters at Standing Rock who valiantly stood down minions of wrongly legislated law as they defended homeland against interlopers.

We are poised on many edges of jeopardy. This is not the time to despair, but rather react with courage and conviction based on fully understanding the consequences of what we choose to do or not to do. Consciousness is Nature's gift to our species. Let us not squander this great gift on paltry endeavors but rather use it in behalf of the greatest good for the biotic community.

And stay relentless.

8. | Counterculture in the Land of Clear Light

This essay originally appeared in El Palacio *(Spring 2008).*

NEW MEXICO—FAIREST OF THEM all. High country, thin air, clear light, drier than a skeleton's sense of humor, sparsely vegetated, sparsely populated, land of multiethnic *mestizaje*, outlaw country, haven for ex-patriots, artists, writers, bohemians, beatniks, and hippies; proving ground for scientists of myriad persuasions; paradise with an edge; a habitat of soul-sculpting wind that either welcomes one or blows one away. For those lucky enough to spend their lives herein, it is homeland, the place above all others that you want to live in, to die in.

For thousands of years, waves of human immigrants have wandered into this harsh but beautiful landscape, at first hunting megafauna for meat, hides for clothing and shelter, and bones for tools. They gathered plants for food and medicinal properties, gradually compiling lore to be recalled in myth and oral traditions that have seeped even into the present. They were spiritually nurtured by chthonic deities with whom ancient ancestors danced, ceremonially invoking their numinous presence in celebration of the spirit of place and ensuring that the seasonal cycles would continue to unfold through time and space within an ever-enduring present.

Gradually, nomadic cultures affixed themselves within their territories and achieved indigeneity. Ancestral Puebloan Indians situated their communities near water and developed agricultural skills that survive into the present. They built structures of rock, wood and mud whose ruins continue to endure the winds of time and retain vast spiritual significance for modern Puebloan Indians who ever seek harmony with the flow of Nature.

Nomadic Athabascans, ancestors of Navajos and Apaches, migrated into the landscape from the north, and challenged the territorial rights of the Puebloans, affirming that conflict is a factor in cultural evolution. And from the south came a wave of new colonists whose mixed ancestry could be traced to the Iberian Peninsula, the Pyrenees Mountains, and North Africa. And from the east arrived yet another wave of so-called "Anglo-Americans," whose ancestors came to cultural consciousness in northern Europe and the British Isles.

Wave after wave of humanity spread across the continent of North America, some pushing to the sea to the west; others beached at the base of a great mountain range presently named the Sangre de Cristo, the blood of Christ, geo-mythically transfused over millennia from Jerusalem.

By the late nineteenth century, the New Mexico Territory was one of the most culturally diverse regions to be found in North America. It was also one of the most dangerous. Outlawry was rampant. The United States was the latest in a succession of nations to claim New Mexico as her own in spite of the presence of autochthonous cultures that had tapped age-long roots deep into the soil from which they drew spiritual sustenance. The United States waged wars on many Indian tribes including Apaches, Navajos, and Comanches who heroically defended their rights to homeland against interlopers who sought to expand the new empire. Bands of outlaws were legion, many of whose members had been US or Confederate soldiers, some of whom had been lawmen, a few of whom switched hats trusting to the inspiration of the moment.

By 1912, as New Mexico entered statehood, the cultural landscape had been tamed in the main. The presence of the railroad made New Mexico accessible from all points. New Mexico was perceived as a health haven for tuberculars, or "lungers" as they were called. The father of author Paul Horgan suffered from tuberculosis and moved his family westward in 1915. In Horgan's own words:

"I was twelve years old when my family removed to Albuquerque from Buffalo, New York, and Albuquerque then was a Río Grande small city of fourteen thousand people. Its main concerns economically were the Santa Fe Railroad, which was a division point and had great shops. The transcontinental line was the lifeblood of the city, going east and west many times a day—many trains a day. It was a local rite to go and visit the arrival of the important train, the California Limited, one east and one westward every day. Celebrities would disembark and stroll the platforms at Albuquerque and visit the Indian exhibits and the Santa Fe—the Fred Harvey establishment with its collection of regional antiques and so forth. So it became a citizen's promenade, really, to go and witness this every day as the great trains went east and west."

During the course of his long life, Horgan went on to write extensively about New Mexico, twice winning the Pulitzer Prize, and for many years participated in the art colony near Roswell that included artists Peter Hurd and Henriette Wyeth. The ancient city of Santa Fe held fascination for many artists and writers including Alice Corbin Henderson, Mary Austin, Wytter Binner, and Haliel Long.

To the north, the village of Taos had long been an intercultural encounter zone for Indians of different tribes, Spanish colonists and their descendants, mountain men, trappers, traders, and adventurers of every ilk. In 1919, the thrice-married bohemian Mabel Dodge Sterne arrived from the east with her husband, Maurice. A Taos Indian, Tony Luhan convinced her to purchase a twelve-acre piece of land where she was to build an adobe mansion. As one story goes, Tony pitched a teepee in front of her original house and drummed nightly until she came to him. Maurice became history, Mabel married Tony in 1923, and the couple lived happily ever after.

Mabel Dodge Luhan's home became a haven for ex-patriots, writers, thinkers, early counterculturalists, anthropologists, musicians, and psychologists. She invited D. H. Lawrence (Lorenzo) and his wife Frieda, Carl Jung (for whom the marriage between Tony and Mabel must have seemed a cultural *coniunctio oppositorum*), Dane Rudyhar,

Spud Johnson, Jaime de Angulo, and myriad others to visit and spend creative time.

In 1924, author and linguist Jaime de Angulo and Tony Luhan became fast friends. Jaime had hoped that Tony would reveal some of the secrets of Taos Puebloan culture that Tony steadfastly refused to divulge. Even though he had been somewhat ostracized from his people because of marrying a white woman, Tony remained loyal to the Taos Puebloan tradition of cultural privacy.

In a conversation recalled by de Angulo, Tony asked, "What for do you want to know? Those things belong to the Indians. They are not for whites. What can the whites do with them? The Indians have got to have them because they do things with them, but the whites want to know just for curiosity."

To which the prescient de Angulo replied, "No, Tony. I don't want to know just for curiosity. I want to know because I think the whites have lost their soul and they must find it again. Some of the things the whites have lost, the Indians have kept."

"Yes," said Tony. "We know the explanation of how everything is . . . We know many things the whites don't know. But I will never tell you."

As Jaime mentioned in his letters to his wives, the Taos Pueblo was comprised of two factions, the traditionalist, and the more recent peyote cult that was criticized by the traditional Puebloans. Immediately to the south of the Pueblo, some fair amount of individual criticism occurred between visitors to Mabel's household. For example, Jaime and D. H. Lawrence made for bad chemistry. Lorenzo openly snubbed Jaime. Jaime characterized Lorenzo as follows:

"Talking of neurotics, that Lawrence is certainly one. . . . [He] is ridiculous as only an Englishman can be ridiculous. His face is a combination of Tolstoy, G. B. Shaw and Abraham Lincoln, very pallid skin, and a semi-bushy semi-goat-like beard. . . . His mental makeup is fully as queer. He has quarreled with everybody under the sun, and I am not surprised. He is clever, keen, biting, with the sensitiveness of a woman, the aggressiveness of a cock, a bad temper, full of insolence, entirely irrational."

In spite of petty interpersonal conflicts, the bohemian tapestry woven by Mabel Dodge Luhan added spectacular coloration to the greater cultural hue even beyond the Southwest. However, the stock market crash of 1929 overshadowed every aspect of American life, and the predominant national hue verged on dark grey. The cities were hardest hit wherein prosperity dwindled, and breadlines wound through city streets. There were long lines of weary Americans awaiting their turn to sleep for a few hours in a protected environment. The cultural countenance reflected desperation. The national theme song was "Brother, Can You Spare a Dime?"

The Great Depression lasted for over a decade, wherein President Franklin D. Roosevelt did everything in his power to reinvigorate economic recovery. His New Deal included funding artists, writers, musicians, and actors to continue to practice their artforms. At the same time, the New Deal funded the Civilian Conservation Corps training and paying young men to spiff up the countryside by rip-rapping arroyos and constructing fire lookout towers. The New Deal also provided funding for great public works projects including the Tennessee Valley Authority.

Nevertheless, it took World War II to provide the major impetus to "rebirth" the American economy. The US government conscripted or lured many scores of thousands of young men to fight the Axis in Europe and the South Pacific. A disproportionately high ratio of young New Mexican Hispanos were drafted and sent off to war never to return, thus hewing a great rent in the fabric of their culture at home. The remaining labor force across America was involved in construction of battleships, warplanes, guns, and ammunition. Rosie the Riveter became the national heroine, and for a time, the song "I'll Be Seeing You," crooned by a youthful Frank Sinatra, wafted across the airwaves from the *Saturday Night Hit Parade* fueling the dreadful poignance that dominated virtually every home in America.

Then we dropped the bomb. And then the second bomb. And then the war was over, and surviving battered and exhausted veterans returned to a new, economically reinvigorated America, the planet's international savior standing firm at the threshold of the atomic age determined to stare down the new threat of communism that dominated the Soviet Union and China. And thus was launched the Cold War that was to last for much of the rest of the twentieth century.

America was also celebrating a brief golden age that included the return of prosperity and a state of undisputed world leadership. However, the newly configured economically dominated cultural paradigm was very restrictive in a sense that deeply affected the perceptions of a few writers, artists, and musicians in post-bohemian havens including Greenwich Village and North Beach.

The late Philip Whalen was one of the great poets to emerge from the Beat generation. For many years, he was both a close friend and my next-door neighbor, and we engaged in conversation almost daily. I recorded Philip addressing his perceptions of the genesis of the Beat scene.

"Well, Beat generation, at this point we have to get very careful and historically accurate and whatnot, and repeat what's in all the textbooks, which is true—that the name was invented by Kerouac to deal with a period in New York after the war, say about 1947. John Clellon Holmes, a friend of Jack's . . . had an assignment to write an article . . . about current American novel writing. So here was this new generation.

"'They used to say that there was a lost generation after the First World War. What could we call where we're at after the Second World War?' Jack said, 'Well, why don't you call it the Beat generation because we're all beat. We're all tired of the war and we don't have any money. Nobody knows who we are. We're just sort of out of everything and we're kind of way out on the fringe somewhere and kind of moping along. So why don't you say Beat generation.'

"So that's where that came from. It dealt, to some degree, with life around the drug scene and high-mopery scene around Times Square in 1947, which involved Burroughs and Corso and Ginsberg and Kerouac and a number of other people."

In 1955, Kerouac's seminal novel, *On the Road*, was first published and helped set a new tone in both American literature and subculture. At about the same time, Allen Ginsberg headed west to the Bay Area and looked up poet Kenneth Rexroth who advised him to get in contact with some of the local poets, including Philip Lamantia, Gary Snyder, and Michael McClure. With the help of several poets, Ginsberg organized a poetry reading to be held at the Six Gallery in San Francisco in October 1955. Gary Snyder contacted his old Reed College housemate, Philip Whalen, who was then on Sourdough Mountain working as a fire lookout and invited him to participate in the reading. At that time, Ginsberg was finishing and polishing a poem that he would read at the forthcoming poetry bash. The poem is titled "Howl."

About 250 people crowded into the small gallery to witness what came to be regarded as a major literary milestone. Lawrence Ferlinghetti immediately asked to publish Ginsberg's "Howl" and thereafter found himself in deep trouble with the feds for publishing what they deemed to be pornography. The truth is, the American establishment was outraged by the myriad fiery truths expressed in Ginsberg's brilliant scathing poem whose opening lines reveal: "I saw the best minds of my generation destroyed by madness, / starving hysterical naked." Jack Kerouac arrived in the Bay Area and befriended poet and orientalist Gary Snyder. They moved into a cabin together in Mill Valley in 1955 and spent quality outdoor time seriously hiking around Mt. Tamalpais and beyond. Thus Gary became the prototype for Japhy Ryder, the rucksack-toting backcountry Zen Buddhist hero of Kerouac's novel, *The Dharma Bums.*

I first arrived in North Beach in the autumn of 1958 after having been discharged from the US Army where I had served as an army bandsman. Most of my military time had been spent in the Mojave Desert at Camp Irwin and part of my time at the Nevada Proving Grounds at Desert Rock. I was a young jazz musician ever more steeped in the primetime jazz that emanated from that era. Part of my Army gig was to play stirring refrains from "The Stars and Stripes Forever," while peers of Dr. Strangelove fired off atomic bombs seven miles from where we bandsmen stood in the predawn desert. One day, back at Camp Irwin, which is located about thirty-five miles from Barstow, Danny the barber and dealer fell by the barracks and said, "You've got to read this! Now!" He handed me the tiny book titled *Howl and Other Poems* by Allen Ginsberg. I devoured the book and ruminated deeply about life in the milieu into which I had been born to which I was commanded to contribute music to celebrate the detonation of atomic bombs. And thus I came to realize that I wasn't the one who was insane.

Footloose at last, I wandered up and down the West Coast from the Lighthouse at Hermosa Beach to the Co-Existence Bagel Shop in North Beach. I played my horn for modest coin of the realm, read in the City Lights Bookstore, watched sunset from the Golden Gate, ate my daily five-course Italian meal for $1.25 that included a half-carafe of wine, visited galleries, one of which displayed the strange collage, *Tribute to Caryl Chessman*, that I believe was crafted by Bruce Conner who would later produce a film that showed one atomic bomb explosion after the other.

Part of the time, I hung out in Big Sur and spent one wonderful evening in the presence of Henry Miller as we all drank wine at Nepenthe. In Sausalito's Gate Five, I befriended the Greek artist Jean Varda, who many years later died as he exited an airplane in Mexico City. It is said that his final words were, "Ah. Instant metaphysics."

During that period of the late 1950s, I hitchhiked across America and passed through New Mexico, to me the most beautiful state-of-mind on Earth. I knew it was my homeland at last discovered, yet it would be four years before I would begin the rest of my life there.

Throughout the 1930s, '40s, and '50s, artists, writers, and skilled artisans moved to New Mexico to fashion their own handcrafted lifestyles. By the 1950s, the talented novelist William Eastlake had settled on his ranch near Cuba, New Mexico, where he wrote his celebrated New Mexico trilogy. Malcolm Brown finely honed his eccentricities in Taos. John DePuy painted his provocative landscapes in Taos while Georgia O'Keeffe painted her masterpieces in and around Abiquiu.

Max Finstein penned poetry. Liz Walker wove god's-eyes after the fashion of the Huichol Indians. Edward Abbey wrote his first novels and briefly earned his keep as a bartender at the Taos Inn where it has been told that one evening, Lady Brett, the great friend of D. H. Lawrence, visited the bar and requested a grasshopper. To which Ed Abbey responded, "Who the hell would drink a grasshopper? I quit!"—much to the dismay of myriad customers who imbibed freely and at little cost thanks to the deft hand of Brother Abbey.

And thus it was that in 1962, a loose-knit coterie of Bay Area post-beatniks, many of whom had read *Indian Tales* by Jaime de Angulo, *Howl* by Allen Ginsberg, *Riprap* by Gary Snyder, *The Way of Zen* by Alan Watts, *Siddhartha* by Herman Hesse, *Tao Te Ching* by Lao Tzu, the *I Ching*, *The Doors to Perception* by Aldous Huxley, *The Lord of the Rings* by J. R. R. Tolkien, and other soul-shaping literature of the era, and who had experienced the exquisite spiritual opening into the flow of Nature by ingesting peyote, and the fascinating alteration of mental processes wrought by smoking marijuana, began to wander into the land of clear light. We too brought with us our handcrafted lifestyles and knew well how to live simply.

Some played and sang folk music; some made sandals; others were jewelry makers; yet others earned their keep washing potshards at the Laboratory of Anthropology or spent months in solitude on top of mountains and high mesas as fire lookouts. Rick and Sue Mallory moved to Mancos, Colorado, and settled into family life raising their children. Alan and Joan Lober opened the Morningbird, a shop that specialized in Indian arts and crafts, and employed their friends. John and Marie Kimmey founded the Santa Fe Community School, an alternative school that catered to the offspring of counterculturalists. Jimmy Hopper ran a tiny restaurant in El Rito before heading into the Gila Wilderness to become a fire lookout atop Mogollon Baldy. Randy Allen sang songs, played the guitar, and became a jeweler. Yvonne Bond pursued radical politics all the way to the island of Cuba. Recluse Jon Sanford printed a poster that advised, "Search for Truth and Honesty in American Politics." Peter Ashwandan became widely recognized as the illustrator of John Muir's classic, *How to Keep Your Volkswagon Alive: A Manual of Step-by-Step Procedures for the Compleat Idiot.* Chris and Cynthia West bought acreage at the top of the Pilar Hill, a pilgrim station that looks out over the magnificent landscape riven by the Río Grande Gorge. Tahiti Gervais practiced the craft of blacksmithy. Dick Brown, a native New Mexican, guided many of us through the multicultural labyrinth that continues to prevail and evolve. Peter VanDresser had lived in New Mexico for many years, and through his wisdom, became the godfather of the alternative energy movement. Max Finstein was a friend to us all.

What bound everyone was an abiding love for the flow of Nature and the intimation that our purpose as humans is to attain the highest level of consciousness possible. And frequently on a Saturday night, a tipi would be pitched on someone's property, and the peyote ritual would be consummated through the night till dawn, sometimes attended by Little Joe Gomez, Tellus Goodmorning, and other Indians from the Taos Pueblo and beyond.

Gradually everyone became affixed to the New Mexican landscape, endlessly enchanted, ever-nurtured by the spirit of place.

The 1960s was indeed a time of flowering of consciousness. The war in Vietnam spawned national outrage. The civil rights movement burst through the dike of cultural repression and spread across America. Three voices of hope—those of Jack Kennedy, Martin Luther King, and Bobby Kennedy—were silenced by assassins. Timothy Leary and Richard Alpert were fired from Harvard University for their experiments with psilocybin, a psychotropic natural substance that would rearrange the mental coordinates of tens of thousands of American youths. Tim coined the dictum: "Turn on, tune in, drop out." Richard transformed into Baba Ram Dass and forwarded his own message in *Be Here Now.* Joan Baez, Bob Dylan, and the Beatles greatly enhanced the listenability of popular music. Carlos Castaneda published his dissertation, *The Teachings of Don Juan,* and though he failed to immediately receive his PhD, he inspired a generation of young Americans to look beyond the narrow boundaries of the monocultural frame of reference and into a fifth dimension where shamans dance and ply their skills. An undercurrent of anarchism spread across the land. Thousands rejected the image of the man in the grey flannel suit, the drear of investing one's lifetime at the corporate behest, the pursuit of wealth for its own sake, of having a job instead of a life. Thus, the hippie movement was launched, directly descended from the Beat scene, itself born from the bohemian countercultural lineage that invigorated Greenwich Village, North Beach, Venice, the Parisian salon of Gertrude Stein, and the New Mexico high country consciousness-compound founded by Mabel Dodge Luhan.

One of the more celebrated city-sites of hippieness occurred in the Haight Ashbury district of San Francisco. These blossomed around the United States and beyond. One of the most profound multifaceted experiments in hippie counterculture occurred in rural northern New Mexico where habitat is illuminated by Sun, Moon, and blossoming stars rather than city lights. It was here that hippie communes sought foothold in the beautifully harsh environments of high desert country where for millennia, humans of myriad cultural persuasions had already tested their mettle, some flourishing, many more withering, all contributing to a human continuum shaped at least as much by habitat as by ideal.

The notion of "commune" began to evolve in medieval Europe a thousand or more years ago when people of similar persuasions and practices constructed walled communities in order to physically defend themselves against the forces of feudal lords and other bandits and to defend their rights as human beings to practice lifestyles that were commensurate with their collective natures. Over the centuries even to the present, many types of communes have dotted the landscapes of Europe, Asia, and the Americas.

The anarchists of nineteenth-century Europe reacted against totalitarian governments that they rejected sometimes to the death. The short-lived Paris Commune of 1871 was the first organized uprising of the proletariat against capitalism. The participants in this social experiment became known as "communards." Anarchism took many forms, but Peter Kropotkin's anarchist communism resonates to this day with many communards who shared time and space in the hippie commune phase of New Mexico's history. Kropotkin defined anarchist society as follows:

"The anarchists conceive a society in which all its members are regulated, not by laws, not by authorities, whether self-imposed or elected, but by mutual agreements between the members of that society, and by a sum of social customs and habits—not petrified by law, routine, or superstition but concordance with the ever-growing requirements of a free life, stimulated by the progress of science, invention, and the steady growth of higher ideals. No ruling authorities, then. No government of man by man; no crystallization and immobility, but a continual evolution—such as we see in Nature."

It is doubtful that more than a handful of New Mexico's hippies ever read these words, and many counterculturalists would not agree with everything that Kropotkin said. For example, one morning Allen Ginsberg and Peter Orlovsky were having breakfast with us in Santa Fe. Allen read Kropotkin's definition that has long been pinned to my studio wall. He took umbrage at Kropotkin's support of science, which led us to a lengthy discussion about the practice of science versus the misapplication of science. Personally, I strongly support scientific research, but rue many of the ways it is applied within the realm of a military/corporate/industrial/political complex committed to acquisition of power for its own sake, and to turning habitat into money in order to gain and retain that power.

Be all of that as it may, northern New Mexico of the mid-1960s was alive with an energy that was palpable, alluring, and ripe for social experimentation. Men and women of great personal energy were lured to the high desert. Some had enough money to buy large tracts of land to be held in common. Others had the vision to found communes on these commons, communes of different flavors but with a common denominator founded in self-direction, mutual aid, and love of the Earth. Another denominator common to many communards was the use of pot, hash, peyote, mescaline, LSD, psychedelic mushrooms, and other substances, some of which had their genesis in laboratories operated by high-minded biochemists. Some of the better known of the more than two dozen New Mexico communes included New Buffalo, Morning Star, Lama, the Hog Farm, and the Reality Construction Company. Taos County became the communal proving ground where at one point the hippie population of the county came in at over 15 percent!

In her worthy publication, *Scrapbook of a Taos Hippie*, published by Cincos Puntos Press, Iris Keltz provides an excellent portrait of the great hippie commune experiment of the late 1960s and early '70s. She relies on her own recollections (and it's NOT TRUE that if you remember the '60s, you weren't there!), excerpts from oral histories that she conducted with tribal members of the countercultural revolution, and articles that appeared in both the *Taos News* and the *Fountain of Light*. This book is generously illustrated with photographs including some by the hippie photo-documentarian, Lisa Law.

Max Finstein turned into one of the great communard visionaries of the 1960s and '70s. He was associated with the Beat generation as a poet and had been a jazz alto sax player. He loved to smoke pot and drink wine, philosophize, and talk far into the night. In the early 1960s, he split with his then wife, left New Mexico, and hit the road with his daughter Rachel. He met a new lady and returned to New Mexico in 1966. He hooked up with Rick Klein, a youngster from Pennsylvania who had happened into a sum of money that he was willing to spend to purchase land on which to found a commune. A one hundred-three-acre piece of land with water rights was found near Arroyo Hondo north of Taos. It was situated both near the Río Grande and a hot springs, and it was for sale for $55,000. Rick popped for the land and shortly thereafter, there was a gathering of hippies who put up a tipi and held a peyote meeting. And thus New Buffalo was born. Rick had this to say about the genesis of New Buffalo.

"I was going to be a literature professor and then I took LSD and saw that there's more to it than just this. There's being with your friends. Culture was very exciting at that time. I had an inheritance, and I bought land in New Mexico and got involved in New Buffalo. The first thing we did was have a peyote meeting, and Max (Finstein) was the roadman. Ultimately, I got very involved with Little Joe Gomez from the Taos Pueblo and his brother John and all those old men up there. The last one just passed away last year. Frank Zamora. He was a hundred years old. Frank had this incredible psychedelic style. They were all exceptional people."

There was no such thing as a hippie-type cookie cutter that stamped out hippie after hippie from a specific hippie gene pool. Hippies emerged as individuals from every conceivable background.

Un-dam the stream of consciousness.
Everyone came from the American melting pot and had reacted
    to the post-Victorian lock on open sexuality that seemed like
    an affront to a natural biological imperative, who wanted to
    escape concrete canyon walls where wind blows cold and dank
    with smoggy humidified fumes emitted
as ghastly emanations from that aspect of the Gaseous Vertebrate
aligned with military Mammon-might reeking of corporate cigar
    breath
spewing forth over innocent new-born, frightening mind-blight
of the politically correct . . .
yaarghh!!
Turn to sunlight, dark night star blossoms, mountain-rimmed
    spirit-land
sweet acrid smoke mix of juniper-piñon-marijuana
wafting up my nose to settle my mind into a clear look into the
    known
perchance to be forgotten, to slide into
cool-hip ever present
Be Here Now-ness of
Turned On-Tuned In-Dropped Out into fanciful magic land
LOVE LOVE LOVE
That's the thing that there's just too little of—

Sweet Jesus! Blessed Bodhisattva mind Krishna flute song
Hanuman happiness Sufi dervish dance
tornado of tipi consciousness
spun-out along a rainbow brain-blow trail
of delight comes at dawn after staring into Morningbird firelight
all night all night all night all night long
singing peyote songs to beat of water drum, dance of feathers fan-
    ning
Road man, drummer, cedar man
Earthmother calling calling calling calling
Sacred water, tipi consciousness At One With All
Begin mud dance straw dance sun dance
Make adobes not bombs in sunlight look to mountain rim for
    God-dance
Clouds
work work work work
play play play play
Naked
Rosy-nippled double-breasted thrashers
Flirting with dawn crowing cocks in flowing bird dance of desire
Making babies, new flesh forms cradles of unblemished con-
    sciousness
To scatter at play in the fields of the Lord
Be rid almost of clichés, almost . . .

There was great work involved in building structures of adobe, gathering
vigas to support roofs, gathering firewood, ever more firewood, endless
gathering of firewood for cooking, heating against breath-frosting winter coldness, life-threatening winter coldness. Four-hole defecation
zone, communal shitholes, no more mind barriers to plug up biological
flow of Nature's manure. Don't eat yellow snow. Don't wash diapers in
the hot spring.

Where does the food come from? Some hunting, gardening, learning the seasons, the cycles, hitting up strangers for bread in town,

some checks from home, food stamps, can't seem to get fully out of tentacles reach of economic kraken that stretches into every corner of human patina-planet overlay pulsing away, fiscal metastasis creeping into soil, sucking away in return for consciousness, or so we hope . . .

Ever more of us dismaying Indigenes—Indians, Chicanos, especially Chicanos now at home determined to defend turf, mores, many taking great umbrage at naked mud dancers throwing away econo-tenets to which everyone else aspires to perfect; relegated since 1846 to shadow culture; forced to reject subsistence existence to attempt to survive the riptides of the American Way of Life. Burn out the *chingados*, beat the *mierde* out of them. Launch a Chicano revolt to rid the land of the hippies and the feds. History repeats itself—remember 1680—Popé was the first great North American revolutionary. Now there was Tijerina—get the feds off the land grants. Don the brown beret. Defend a lingering way of life whose soul-lore was diminished in World War Two at Bataan. *¡Tierra o muerte!*

It wasn't all bad with the Chicanos. Rick Klein recalls a time when hippies maintained some of the responsibilities normally held by Hispanos.

"Obviously it was very threatening because of the press, and words like sex and drugs, and stuff like that. The Hispanos were feeling marginalized and losing their traditions. Nobody wanted to be the mayordomo of the ditch (acequia), and for years the mayordomo of the ditch in Arroyo Hondo was from New Buffalo. They (the Hispanos) had to have some respect for us. We were working hard. People would come to my house and say, 'This is just like my grandfather's.'"

There was a flowering of consciousness that required extreme hippieness to regenerate, propagate, linger within long enough to endure before the short-lived Age of Aquarius wafted into what was to become. The communes, each with its own distinct collective character, blossomed and contended as best the communards could, most, like adobe, melting back into the cultural soil of the land of clear light. By virtue of their lifestyle which included practices deemed illegal by the law of the land, they became and remained outlaws and practitioners of Walt Whitman's now famous apothegm, "Resist Much. Obey Little."

There were hardworking men and women who poured their souls into the experiment. Others, who were previously deeply damaged by circumstances from without and within, were nurtured back to sanity. Some died. Others achieved extraordinary spiritual heights. There were attempts at alternative education. John Kimmey and others brought their talents and skills to bear on educating the young into a new world consciousness. Many of the children of the great experiment look back in wonder, some with rejection, some with truly expanded consciousness, no one unaffected.

Max Finstein left New Buffalo and traveled all the way to Israel to experience life on a kibbutz where his sphere of reference was expanded yet again within a collective new Israeli point of view that required success if death were to be avoided. A more militant Max returned to New Mexico and helped establish the Reality Construction Company whose members included Chicano activists and angry Afro Americans.

Steve and Barbara Durkee had traveled from upper New York State to found Lama, a commune that has undergone many permutations yet continues to endure. Originally founded as a patriarchal subculture, Lama became a spiritual center that involved many well-known and celebrated passers-through who left their mark in mysterious ways. Baba Ram Dass spent many a night on New Mexican soil, charming seeds of individual consciousness into self-recognition. Stewart Brand contributed his energy to the genesis of Lama and thereafter published the *Whole Earth Catalog* for which he received the National Book Award in 1972. Durkee went on to found Dar al Islam, a Muslim community situated on the other side of the Río Chama from Abiquiu.

David Pratt wended eastward from a commune in central California known as Morningstar West, and with Michael Duncan, who owned part of a mesa top north of Taos, founded Morningstar East, a commune that was populated in large measure by your tired, your poor, your wasted who yearned to be whole and free. Morningstar East and the Reality Construction Company were neighboring communes between which peace and love were tempered with animosity and conflict. There were hard times as well as good times.

Wavy Gravy and the Hog Farmers founded yet another commune south of Peñasco known as the Hog Farm. They were a peripatetic lot who scooted about the nation in their bus (of several incarnations) preserving the peace at hippie gatherings and Be-ins that included the great event that put Woodstock on the map.

Tom Law introduced Yogi Bhajan to New Mexico and New Mexico to Yogi Bhajan who founded a Sikh community near Española that endures to this day.

Hippie culture was not restricted to the communes. Some hippies were more loners than communalists and preferred to camp out in solitude, smoke a joint, and relax into the flow of Nature without necessarily being motivated to make a statement. Some would occasionally wander into a desert hinterland, fast for a few days, and then at dawn ingest peyote buttons after having carefully picked off as much lophophoran as possible to make for a smoother ride through the stomach. As the day unfolded, reality would be revealed in exquisite living glory, the face of rocks dancing, the molecules of existence arranging themselves in such a way that the pilgrim was included in the beauty and wonder and glory of the Spirit of Nature, forever imbued with a sense of spiritual purpose, never again to be restricted to the linear thinking that excludes so much of the great mystery.

While many of the communes withered with the passage of the seasons, and hippies ripened into middle and late age, many found themselves ready to take their knowledge and understanding into the greater culture and to become counterculture activists. John Nichol's superb New Mexico trilogy conveys with great insight the intercultural struggles, both the light and the dark, that characterize human presence in the mythic landscape of northern New Mexico. By the early 1970s, environmental consciousness was flickering into public awareness. Many became inspired by reading *Desert Solitaire*, a great classic penned by Edward Abbey who melded anarchist thought with environmentalism and who thus became the godfather of the radical environmental movement.

In part, hippie consciousness expanded and conjoined with intellect, and a new wave of counterculturalists entered the fray armed with university training in biology, geography, ecology, environmental law, and other disciplines required if humanity is to forestall our own folly. Hippie consciousness also entered the marketplace where organic produce, meat and poultry provide physical sustenance unburdened with additives, pesticides, and preservatives. Clothing styles have become more free, exotic, and comfortable. Hair comes and goes at the whim of the mind inside the head. Music has imploded and exploded carrying every message to every quarter.

There is a growing tendency to perceive from within a sphere of reference filled with clusters of associated notions, experiences, understandings, learnings, through which the active mind may extrapolate future probabilities and possibilities. In pre-hippie days, this form of "ecolate thinking" (a term coined by Garrett Hardin) was not particularly prevalent.

Today, cultural boundaries have been breached, and hippieness is revealed to have cast its hue everywhere. New Mexico remains a many-faceted countercultural proving ground fraught with dangerous edges for the close-minded. But for those with eyes to see, it remains the land of clear light.

9.   In Praise of Restoration Ecology

This essay originally appeared in Green Fire Times *(March 2012).*

AS I WROTE ABOUT in an earlier chapter, in 2009, I produced a documentary radio program titled, "Aldo Leopold in the Southwest." In my travels, I met Estella Leopold, youngest of the five children spawned by Aldo Leopold and Estella Luna Bergere Leopold, herself a native of Santa Fe and a member of the revered Luna family that have lived in New Mexico for many generations. Estella, the younger, is one of America's most distinguished paleobotanists, now professor emerita at the University of Washington in Seattle. She is also a wonderful folk musician whose repertoire includes dozens of Hispano folksongs recalled and sung by her family when she was a child.

When I recorded my interview with her in her home in Seattle, she recounted tales of her childhood that helped characterize her father and mother, both of whom were wildly intelligent, deeply sensitive human beings whose commitment to family generated a model of conduct to which we should all aspire with mighty resolve. As we sat at her dining room table, Estella recounted the following recollection about how the seven members of the Leopold family reacted to the farm with its shack that Aldo Leopold bought in Sand County, Wisconsin, where he wrote much of his magnum opus, *A Sand County Almanac.*

"When we first got there it was probably a cold spring day. We had to drive around through the cornfield to get to the shack because the main road was under water and cold as heck. We got there and there was about three feet of manure in the corner of the cabin. We looked around and it was very bleak, lots of burrs. It was very open wasteland. The farmer had gone broke putting in corn after corn and left for Texas. And Dad got it for taxes at eight dollars an acre. So we got there and Mother looked around and said 'Aldo, are you sure you want to bring the children up here?' And Dad said something like, 'Yeah, we're going to plant all this stuff. Put pinery up there on the ridge and put prairie out on the cornfield and won't that be wonderful?' And so it was. It was great. So we began work on the shack and it became our home away from home. No utilities, just our pump, and the Parthenon—the privy—down the way on the edge of the riverbank. Well, it was the edge of a terrace.

"We were there every weekend all the way through the thirties and the forties—just about every weekend. Absolutely lovely. We built the fireplace, and we fixed the roof and we put in windows and screens. Finally we put in a floor because we had a clay floor first. Mother said we had to fix that, so we did. We had bunks. We had a great time up there. We were doing restoration ecology, which was the beginning of restoration ecology. We put prairie plants into the cornfield and after a while there were enough weeds and these plants that we could burn it off. We set fire to it, and right away the grasses began to expand because as the flames would come upwind, the grass would drop over behind the flames and drop the seeds on the fertilized ash and produce new plants. Pretty soon it became a tall grass prairie. It was wonderful.

"Then we began adding flowering plants to that prairie. But right now the deer get those and it's pretty hard to maintain that because you really need to live there and have a dog there all the time to keep the deer off. Otherwise, you get what we have, which is a tall grass prairie. But at Nina's [her elder sister's] house where the dogs are, there're many, many flowers. There are two hundred and fifty native species in that prairie, so it's a gorgeous garden of flowers every spring and summer. It's just marvelous."

This is one of my favorite stories of thousands that I've recorded over the last half-century because it contains elements necessary to not only heal habitat but also heal our badly broken culture, especially as we try to peer through the opacity that clouds our view into the immediate future.

Aldo Leopold came to the American Southwest in 1909 as a young forest ranger. Over the following years, he wandered by horse through the forest regions of the New Mexico and Arizona territories (they wouldn't become states till 1912). He observed massive soil erosion and gradually came to attribute much of that to overgrazing by cattle and sheep and to the presence of wagon trails carved through an arid landscape subject to seasonal torrential rains. Years later, he applied his growing ecological perspective to the farmer-burnt eighty acres that he had bought in Wisconsin and thus, with the help of his family, initiated the practice of restoration ecology.

While Aldo Leopold may well have been the first within the context of Western culture to practice restoration ecology in America, he was certainly not the first to enhance habitat in the New World. Here in the Southwest, there are examples of habitat enhancement that extend into antiquity among cultures such as the Hohokam with their irrigation canals in the Sonoran Desert of yore, the Río Grande Puebloans with water catchment systems that restore water to aquifers, the Hopis with carefully selected multiple breeds of corn that work within the arid habitat of the Hopi mesas, the Zunis with their waffle gardens, and the Hispanos with their acequia systems, and recognition of water and land as common resources that must not be privatized for financial profit.

Part of Aldo Leopold's genius was to comprehend the potential of ailing land abandoned by a farmer who had egregiously overworked the soil, then study the surrounding habitat to identify the Indigenous plant and animal life, then invigorate a family practice of restoration ecology that not only reinstated health of habitat, but instilled in every family member an understanding of the interrelatedness of every aspect of the biotic community and the absolute need for a system of ethics that includes the land as well as ourselves and other species within our cultural purview.

The profundity of this lesson is of such vast importance today that should we not heed its wisdom, and contemplate its implications, we may fail to veer from our present course to disaster.

Restoration ecology is currently the next necessary step beyond conservation. In a way, President Franklin D. Roosevelt attempted to employ a myriad of the unemployed during the Great Depression of the 1930s by creating the Civilian Conservation Corps (CCC) to create rip-rap in arroyos to retard erosion, build fire-lookout towers, replant seedlings in the wake of the onslaught of the timber industry, and other modes of conduct that he regarded as vital for restoring a failed economic system, and aligning that with an attempt to ensure future health of the natural environment. He also reinvigorated the arts by funding artists of every persuasion to pursue their creative vision. Thus, Roosevelt sought means to recreate the handcrafted lifestyles that harkened back to the earliest days of young America when people worked rather than held down jobs.

Leopold took this a giant step farther by putting the land first and involving his family in its ecological restoration in a fashion that each family member not only adopted his perspective as their own, but went on to evolve a collective body of work that remains an unprecedented contribution to a culture of practice that is itself culturally restorative in the broader sense that restoration ecology and cultural restoration may be perceived as mutually inclusive, each vital to the other. And implicit in this clearly definable culture of practice is the de-secularization of habitat, the re-sacralization of homeland.

Restoration ecology in conjunction with cultural restoration and re-sacralization of homeland must be enshrined as fundamental to our greater human culture of practice. How this is accomplished is up to each individual. It must certainly occur from within the grassroots of human culture; it lies beyond the ken of today's corporate dominated political systems that are proven antithetic to this way of being. Many if not most of today's institutions are based on economic growth for its own sake, a principle that must be redefined.

Somehow, we must collectively foster a paradigm founded in a form of expanded consciousness that includes restoration of habitat, hard work on behalf of the greater good for the entire biotic community, and satisfaction with return to a handcrafted lifestyle shaped by evolving imagination assisted by appropriate science and technology that is harmonious with the flow of Nature—all within a world of diminishing resources. This is a tall order in today's political milieu that has shifted from that of a young, exuberant democracy of two-and-a-half centuries past, to the plutocracy that currently presides. Our collective body politic is antithetic to the environmental standards that we must assume if we are to wend our way through the stormy times that have already befallen.

In 1969, the National Environmental Policy Act was passed by both the Senate and House of Representatives of the Congress of the United States and was signed into law by President Richard M. Nixon on January 1, 1970. Its purpose appears in the preamble as follows:

"To declare a national policy which will encourage productive and enjoyable harmony between man and his environment; to promote efforts which will prevent or eliminate damage to the environment and biosphere and stimulate the health and welfare of man; to enrich the understanding of the ecological systems and natural resources important to the Nation; and to establish a Council on Environmental Quality."

Since 1970, the human population of our planet has nearly doubled. Our species' perceived needs have grown proportionately. We abide within an economic system based on limitless growth. Our natural resources dwindle in direct proportion to our growth, and today, economics overshadows sound ecology by magnitudes within the zeitgeist of modern global culture. In our quest for natural resources, we have left a wake of devastation through natural habitats vital for the maintenance of a viable biotic community. We have committed an immense number of fellow species to extinction. We have created a body of law that erodes our National Environmental Policy Act, an accrual of laws designed to define and defend the Policy of Limitless Growth that our capitalist system demands.

What a de-spirited legacy we are embedding in collective human consciousness. By celebrating the privatization of common pool resources for financial gain, we have gone un-Natural.

What can we do?

First, we must individually and collectively ingest the level of jeopardy to which we have exposed not just ourselves, but the entire biotic community. Then we must determine the wellspring of the calamity, part of which resides in each and every one of us. Then, within the realm of regional and national politics, identify that which serves the greatest good for the entire biotic community, and reject that which does not, honestly critiquing elected officials within our current two-party system where truths are hidden in the shadows of hyperbolic rhetoric. Then we must vote accordingly.

Secondly, we must individually and collectively look to our respective homelands and seek both where jeopardy lies and what homeland itself indicates to be the path to balance within. This is precisely what Aldo Leopold did on the family eighty-acre farm in Sand County.

Third, we look to science to reveal and evaluate our state of peril and for the technology that is most applicable for our endeavor. Science is an essential tool for determining the truth, and its correct application is required if we are to clear the hurdles that lie immediately before us. However, although science is necessary for complete perspective, it alone will not save us from ourselves.

Fourth, after strengthening both our perspective and resolve as bulwarks vital for maintaining the state of mind and discipline necessary for the task at hand, we may then initiate restoration ecology as a culture of practice and in so doing allow ourselves to celebrate our cultural restoration as well, as we consciously realign ourselves with habitat. Thus, we re-sacralize homeland.

The requirements for success include adopting a bioregional perspective from within which to operate as we intelligently proceed as restorers of homeland to ecological balance. For this, we can take a mighty cue from our Puebloan neighbors who continue to survive in relative cultural tact as they have for centuries. We can look to traditional Hispano culture in the northern Río Grande watershed as a model of survivability and resilience relative to homeland. We can support local farmers' markets and food cooperatives wherein sound ecological practices are revealed in the arrays of homegrown foods in which we delight. A fine source of bioregional theory may be found in Gary Snyder's superb book, *The Practice of the Wild.*

Fifth, we can only succeed by initiating a meaningful level of decentralization of political power relative to national and regional governing bodies that are largely under the sway of corporate economics. This may require civil disobedience. It may indeed involve a level of homeland protection that is not to be confused with Homeland Security. We must ever bear in mind that present political legislation often rules in favor of economics over health of habitat. In that sense, human law and natural law are frequently at loggerheads.

If all of this seems overwhelming and beyond one's ken, one can plant some tomatoes, set out water for the birds, and write a poem—and empower one's self to interpret the voices of homeland in juxtaposition with what one reads in the *Times* or hears during the *News Hour.*

————

ONE OF THE most self-empowered fellow humans I'm privileged to know is Melissa Savage, a true friend of over fifty years who, during the 1960s counterculture movement selected to become a deep environmental activist. She went on to get a PhD in biogeography, taught at UCLA where she is now professor emerita, founded the Four Corners Institute in Santa Fe and has spent many years restoring river otters to the wild, both in North America and far beyond. She has expressed great admiration for Dave Foreman, a founder of Earth First! and more recently, the Rewilding Institute. She thinks holistically with regard to the planetary commons and continues to work vigorously at restoration ecology.

Melissa Savage: "Where the commons works is where people are of a mind about the fate of the environment. And only in the past few years have certain things been talked about broadly, for example in North America things like ecosystem services. The recognition, the broad consensus that watersheds provide something for all of us, that we can't just make private hay out of them because we need them. We need them to be intact. I'm so impressed with the shift in consensus. I think global climate change has really pushed this into a new gestalt, a new way of thinking about where we are, who we are.

"Of course the down side of commons is the overuse. So you have to have an agreement and this is difficult to get. We have an extremely diverse society and we have a somewhat polarized society as we all know, politically speaking. So the task is really to somehow have everyone recognize what's at stake in a commons: the air, the water. The fact that global climate change is going to completely change precipitation patterns and what that means to people. Talk about natural processes—global climate change is just a natural process. It's actually happened many times in the earth's history, and it's happening now but it's our doing. Of course we have all these institutions, all these common institutions in place based on what's been going on for hundreds of years. We count on it raining X amount for our agriculture. If that doesn't focus us, if that doesn't start to create a better consensus about what the commons is—obviously not North America, not the Southwest, not the region: the globe. The globe is a bioregion, and what people do in one place has an incredibly strong teleconnection to other places.

"Things like restoration, as with the otters there's just tremendous enthusiasm for it. If people can feel that there's something positive that they can do in the face of the kind of crisis that we're in globally, then they are more than happy to jump aboard and do whatever they can. The support for restoration has been huge.

"It's a shift that's happening kind of across the board. In a way it's a response to the bad news. The news is pretty bad, and I think as resilient human beings you think, well, so what are the options? Not only individually in our own attitude of optimism or pessimism, but across our communities and across our bioregions and across nations. Even across the international community, I think there's a feeling of 'We must do something now. This is our commons and we really have to move into a different mode.'

"I think that underlying the idea of natural process is the idea that these are self-driver, self-wilding as Dave Foreman would say, processes. This is not something that human beings are doing. This is something that natural systems do naturally. I think there's no one who understands this better than Native Americans, and the shift that I see which I'm extremely grateful for, is that people are not speaking for the Native Americans as much as they used to. They're not saying 'This is the Tewa point of view.' Instead they're saying 'Excuse me, could you come to our panel? Could you come to our conference? We want to hear your voice.' You more and more see Pueblo people speaking out on their own view. I think we have to see a lot more of that.

"It's such a very different perspective. I don't even feel that I begin to grasp their point of view. It's certainly about deep time. It's about time on a different scale altogether than we think about. In a way they're connected with natural processes that went on thousands of years ago in a way that with all our reconstructions and restorations are not. So it's really a wonderful thing that they are becoming part of the conversation in a more active way."

———

THE LEVEL OF self-discipline required of each of us as we proceed into the coming decade is profound. We must literally begin by becoming well informed, well read, and well motivated. The Internet is a tool of extraordinary magnitude that may be used successfully in behalf of home habitat. But it must be visited judiciously and not overused. Rather, we must spend as much time as we can out-of-doors swimming in the flow of Nature, working to restore habitat while contemplating the Great Mystery that urged life and consciousness into being on this lovely planet Earth warmed by our Sun—grateful for our brief link with Eternity. . . .

10. | Nature Abhors a Maximum

This essay originally appeared in Green Fire Times *(November 2018).*

IN 1984, I HAD the good fortune to spend part of a day with Dr. Garrett Hardin, the eminent human ecologist who had recently gone emeritus at UC Santa Barbara. My fascination with the notion of "the commons" had begun to burgeon when I read Hardin's classic essay *The Tragedy of the Commons* in 1970. And now I had the opportunity to interview this thinker who inevitably put a new twist on cultural perspectives, almost on a daily basis. Indeed he began by describing his thinking that resulted in his essay. But shortly, he alluded to a phrase that caught my immediate attention—"Nature abhors a maximum." I asked him to expand on that thought, and he replied:

"Well, that's a rather subtle idea, and I never realized the importance of it until a very unusual political scientist named William Ophuls pointed it out. This was his phrase, that 'nature abhors a maximum.' And what he meant by it was this: that if you settle on a single measure of excellence, such as profit in a profit-and-loss system, and decide you're going to maximize the profit no matter what, you can be quite sure that before you get through you will have minimized some other value that you hadn't thought of, but which you really have high regard for. So the idea is, don't be so one-minded as to try to maximize any one thing. But instead, say here's a whole mixture of things I would like to have. Profit is one of them. Also, you would like to have beautiful scenery; you would like to have some wild animals, some wildlife, some wilderness areas, and so on; and you cannot maximize all at once. What you have to do is to agree on some sort of weighted system. How much do you want wilderness? How much do you want profits? How much do you want oil and gas out of the ground? You have to agree on limits for all of those, and that's hard to do. That's a political problem, but you have to try. And if you can agree on how to weight these things, then you can develop a compound measure that would be safe to maximize. Now that is very difficult; nevertheless, that's the way you have to go. Don't maximize a single variable. That's Ophul's message."

So let's consider a variation on this theme.

Using Hardin's example, it seems that "acquiring profit" has been maximized as the capstone of the corporate/political system that has come to prevail in America and beyond. In his superb book, *The Capitalism Papers: Fatal Flaws of an Obsolete System*, Jerry Mander describes how members of the nations that comprised the Allied Forces against the evil Axis during World War II, gathered at Bretton Woods in New Hampshire to create what would become the new global economy and the World Bank. They used television, the captivating new medium of choice to spread the word through advertising that consumerism and economics comprised the culture of practice that would sustain not just America, but the whole world.

The fatal flaw? This brand of capitalist economics is based largely on continuous extraction of nonrenewable natural resources in a world dominated by the human species whose population continues to grow and grow and grow to the extent that at the present time, it would not take just one, but two planet Earths to sustain our continuing growth. Then four planets and more planets as our species depletes the resources and grinds down the biotic community of this planet Earth that spawned life and gave birth to us and resulted in our consciousness.

In a word, we have maximized capitalism as the culture of practice within our commons of human consciousness, and thus concurrently minimized our regard for the planet that sustains us. Within this present cultural perspective, it is politically correct and expedient to hold Nature in contempt. Our legislation increasingly violates natural law. If indeed Nature abhors a maximum, what may we deduce?

That Nature will spit us out. Our living planet Earth will gradually evolve a different biotic community where our species will not be welcome, a biotic community within which consciousness as we know it may be deemed a liability rather than an asset.

This is a profound realization!

There are those of us who love our planet Earth, who skinny-dip in the flow of Nature on a daily basis, who deplore the current state of human events, who despise violence, who weary of the level to which anthropocentrism has enshrouded the commons of human consciousness. There are those of us who realize that we are but one of millions of living fellow species, that we share membership in myriad ecosystems, themselves assemblies of cognition that surround the surface of our planet in an Earthly biosphere.

Biosphere: our living sphere of reference. What does this really mean, not just to us, but to itself? Well, what it means to me at least is that science is gradually acknowledging that life and cognition are two aspects of the same phenomenon. As I've mentioned in earlier essays, the brilliant Chilean biologist Humberto Maturana forwards the notion that "living systems are cognitive systems and living as a process is a process of cognition. This statement is valid for all organisms, with or without a nervous system."

This is available to us intuitively. I have many friends and acquaintances scattered throughout the American West and Mexico who have spoken freely to me of their abiding sense of kindredness with not just all living things, but also the rocks, the water, the air. This understanding is not limited to the so-called Indigenous peoples native to their respective homelands, but also so-called "contemporary" citizens of our living planet, Earth.

I once recorded author Edward Abbey saying: "I regard the invention of monotheism and the other-worldly God as a great setback for human life. Once we took the gods out of Nature, out of the hills and forests around us, and made all those little gods into one great god up in the sky somewhere in outer space, why then human beings, particularly Europeans began to focus our attention on transcendental values, transcendental deity which led to a corresponding contempt for Nature and the world which supports and feeds us. From that point of view, I think that Indians and most traditional cultures had a much wiser world view, in that they invested every aspect of the world around them—all of Nature—animal life, plant life, the landscape itself, with gods, with deity. In other words, everything was divine in some way or other. Pantheism probably led to a much wiser way of life, more capable of surviving over long periods of time."

Ed went on to say, "More and more, we [modern humans] try to solve our problems by submitting to some sort of technological rationalization, which includes the expansion of the industrial system onto the Moon and the rest of the galaxy and God knows where. No wonder all the bodies in the heavenly universe seem to be flying away from planet Earth, according to some astronomers. They're trying to flee this plague of domination and greed."

Ed Abbey had a wondrous imagination, and he was also gifted both intellectually and intuitively. He told me many times that he longed for that state of mind that could only occur when he was one on one with the flow of Nature.

There is a growing coterie of humans beaming into "natural mindedness," thus reinvigorating the commons of human consciousness. It is up to us to "develop a compound measure which it would be safe to maximize," a perspective to subvert the deadly system of cultural coordinates that currently holds us in sway. Abbey said that "either everything is divine, or nothing is." I personally opt for the former. This involves intuition as well as intellect. It seems that Western culture has sublimated that intuitive sense of the divine in Nature by focusing on industrialism, technology, and capitalism for human ends to the exclusion of the rest of the biotic community.

It also seems to me that reawakening our intuition to the sense of the divine in Nature is prerequisite to establishing a foundation for determining the combination of factors within the "compound measure" to maximize as the basis for a new culture of practice. To intuitively heed the wisdom of those "technicians of the sacred" who appear from time to time on every continent in every Indigenous culture, while concurrently intellectually identifying the factors that must be addressed—NEED TO BE ADDRESSED—and then be reincorporated into the commons of human consciousness is our current cultural imperative. Our present prevailing system of attitudes is absolutely out of synch with reality.

This shift in cultural attitude cannot be mandated from on high. It must be nurtured from within the grassroots, from the bottom up by the likes of you and me. We must present a combined front—not as antagonists or conspirators, but as fellow humans united by a common bond founded on recognition of the principles of Nature that include mutual cooperation as fundamental. Compassion is an attribute to which we must constantly aspire. I include a list of factors that need be addressed imminently. The first five were forwarded over four decades ago by Donella and Dennis Meadows in their book, *Limits to Growth*. Others I've garnered from common sense. The former include: human population, food production, industrialization, pollution, and consumption of nonrenewable resources. Further considerations include: world war, pandemic, economic collapse, cyber-collapse, and climate change and climate instability. This is indeed a mighty "compound measure" to contemplate and maximize, and could readily divide our collective attention. But attending to these factors as an integrated system must supplant the corporate/political hostile takeover of the commons of human consciousness.

This is a tall measure. Its complexity is mind-numbing until we perceive it as a complete system. Even then it may seem daunting, but we have to train ourselves in "systems thinking" which actually comes naturally. The reductionist approach should only be applied after we gain a deeper sense of the bigger picture. The bigger picture becomes ever more clarified when we recognize that we have had enlightened scientists including Lynn Margulis, Gary Paul Nabhan, Melissa Savage, Fritjof Capra, and Suzanne Simard to help guide the way to the scientific perception of wholeness. We are blessed with our Indigenous neighbors whose cultural premises are founded in recognition of the sacred nature of homeland. Here in the North American Southwest, we have a longstanding tradition of artists, writers, musicians, green bohemians, fellow naturists, and thinkers of myriad persuasions, many of whom have spent their lives piercing the veils of political hypocrisy and confronting Nature's reality naked and unafraid. We live in a homeland so sweet that it protects us as we are assailed by the human folly that is revealed to us in the daily media. We are already creating many working responses to the problems listed above.

Do we have both the consciousness and collective will to change course? Yes, indeed we do! We are part of Nature's great coterie of fellow creatures, fellow organisms, and it is from this aspect of the flow of Nature that we draw courage and spirit to proceed in behalf of life and consciousness.

I frequently hearken to the poetry of the late Robinson Jeffers when I've gazed over long into the eye of the storm. Thus, I include the concluding lines of Jeffers poem, "The Answer":

Integrity is wholeness, the greatest beauty is
Organic wholeness, the wholeness of life and things, the divine
beauty of the universe. Love that, not
Man apart from that, or else you will share man's pitiful confu-
sions,
or drown in despair when his days darken.

11. | A Sonoran Illumination

This essay originally appeared in Wild Earth *(Spring 1993).*

I AM HIDING. HOPEFULLY, the silhouettes of the nearby blooming saguaros and yellow-flowered palos verdes disguise my motionless shape. Sweat is dripping into my eyes even though our Mother Earth has yet to tilt this aspect of her membrane out of the shadows cast by the volcanic range east of me. The Sun is not yet visible however its light has aroused the prevailing community of diurnal creatures from slumber. All around me, I hear voices. Only I am silent, empty, receptive to the evidence of my senses. My predominant sense, hearing, is acute. Nearest me is a Gambel's quail calling to the dawn in a mid-high pitch of sound, a single call uttered randomly, frequently, whimsically. Beyond the sound of the quail, I hear a call I know to issue from a cactus wren. In the same range is the more mellifluous call of the curve-billed thrasher. The greater panoply includes two phainopeplas; the voices of mourning doves blending with the voices of white-winged doves, both nearby; the distant voices of Gila woodpeckers who scream into the brightening day; the random warm tones of hummingbirds' wings; more scattered quail fading beyond my range; the ubiquitous hum of thousands of insects' wings whose dynamic range fluctuates to my ear. Now the owls are silent, the coyotes still, although earlier, the elf owls and coyotes yipped in chorus.

I have held this same position throughout the dawn. I have not moved except to breathe, as silently and motionlessly as I can. I have remained hidden, although my presence is known and registered throughout the prevailing community. I am a human, a visitant—an interloper perhaps, but not an enemy. In hiding, but without anxiety or fear, concerned only that I disturb this prevailing community as little as possible as I listen to the collective voices of its denizens. I have amplified my hearing by at least 300 percent. I am listening through headphones as I digitally record the sounds of the Sonoran Desert in stereo. I am hearing creatures in relation to each other rather than as isolated species. These creatures represent the collective consciousness of a biotic community that characterizes the basin known currently to humans as the Ajo Valley. I have just camped the night in Kuakatch Wash. From my vantage as I face south, I can see the Ajo Range to my left and the Bates Mountains to my right. To the south is an alluvial plain, a bajada, a desert membrane as rich with life as any desert in the world. A perfect environment, a meld of biota cradled by prevalent landforms, an ecosystem characterized by geophysical and biological forms which have co-evolved in a state of mutual interdependence to found a bioregion, an entity unto its own now ten thousand years old.

How many species are currently at home here?

How many species pass through?

How long does it take to recover when a wave of "exotics" descends, stays, then moves on?

Indigenous man has been at home here longer than the life of the Sonoran bioregion, or so is indicated by the presence of Clovis points and sleeping circles of stone. But is monocultured man at home without the endless accoutrement, the attendant energy? Monocultured man—monotheistic, driven by techno-lust, isolated from the sense of natural habitat, perhaps collectively insane by now in the face of evidence that we may be nothing more than a malignant bloom metastasizing throughout the mosaic of life. But with a consciousness possibly capable of understanding the physical characteristics of the universe, of visualizing its primordial stuff, of listening to echoes of the primal explosion which burst forth with matter into the continuum of space and time . . .

Time to speculate now. Time to regroup.

What does the evidence indicate to someone bereft of enough common sense to seek shelter from the light of the Sun that has revealed his hiding place? This white-haired, white-bearded eccentric who insists on listening to and recording birds and bugs in the wild in the hope of understanding the common language, the words in the chorus, the collective expression of existence in response to the urge to exist?

"Good question, *frijol viejo*," says the ghost he senses by his side— whom he wishes were sitting there in the flesh, whose recorded thoughts were at least as relevant as those of any other human, and who sat just there off and on over the years.

Until recently, the solar system was the largest ecosystem I could safely imagine. But then I saw a picture, an artist's rendering of the universe in red, white, and blue (no slam intended), and my meager imagination made a quantum leap. Now it seems perfectly clear that the universe is the parent eco-system. There's time enough in a billion years or so to speculate as to what urge gave birth to the knowable universe whose provenance was a microdot—a dense compaction of energy and potential for matter, space, and time.

"Maybe God comes at the end of the universe," whispers this ghost by my side.

I have to consider this.

But first I have to shed a few biases. Like Judeo-Christian-Islamic traditions. Like Brahma-Vishnu-Krishna traditions. Or even the Buddha mindset. Be rid of anthropomorphisms, if just for a little while—long enough to see a tree, or a desert, or the space between the stars. Rid myself of economics, "the law of the land," the system of mores into which I was born. Pull all the nails out of my frame of reference. Rid myself of everything including my sense of self, as best I can. Be rid of my concept of Nature, my sense of Tao. Eradicate the mythic process from my being. Decongest my frontal lobes. Empty myself of all preconceptions and try, with all my will, to become a tabula rasa.

And then try to imagine entering death in this state of mind—with this kind of honesty and resolve.

"That's what it takes," murmurs my buddy's ghost.

Be rid of my buddy's ghost.

Now what? I am still conscious. Take stock. Do I feel rapport with this place and its denizens? Am I related by some common denominator? Is there a fundamental tie between this organic entity in which my mind presides and this semi-arid place where I crouch? How far does it extend? What are the shared characteristics?

Many of the fauna here, in this desert, this bioregion, this planet, have more or less the same sensory apparatus as I. My territory has been invaded. A red ant is biting my ankle. I flick it off, hoping I haven't injured it. I feel empathy for the ant, for the organic creatures, floral and faunal. This empathy extends to the place itself that I perceive to be an integrated system with a consciousness of its own that is comprised of a collective sensory apparatus constrained within the prevailing biota of which I am a member.

I am a member of a biotic collective. No more. No less. This is now a fundament of my consciousness. And to a certain extent, probably far more than I realize, this is understood as fundamental to the coalesced consciousness of this biotic collective. Does this consciousness extend beyond the biota to include the inorganic? In truth, I cannot say. However, my intuitions respond affirmatively. Are my intuitions adequate to be trusted? Again, I do not know.

For a while, thinking stops as I observe without reflection. Life feeds on life. I hear it, see it happening—taste it, feel it, smell it. Entropy. Yet life, evolution, seemingly favors the complex.

It comes to me that life and consciousness are in some way a response to the very urge that gave birth to the universe. Seems reasonable. Scattered throughout the universe there must be myriad circumstances of similar consciousness. And dissimilar consciousness. Is it possible that the universe is home to a seemingly infinite number of collective consciousnesses whose bodies are of equal number? Is each life-bearing planet like a single brain cell complete with an encoded transcript of its experience of existence? What of non-life-bearing planets? Or solar systems? Or galaxies? Or galactic clusters?

Perhaps the universe is a single entity, an organism, itself evolving to accommodate a single idea, a single thought comprised of all the data recorded by all the biota, and quasi-biota, and non-biota that exist, have existed or will exist—an idea thirty billion years and fifty-nine sextillion miles long—an idea that is completed at the moment the universe collapses in on itself in a monstrous implosion.

"Whose idea was it, anyway?" mutters the ghost by my side.

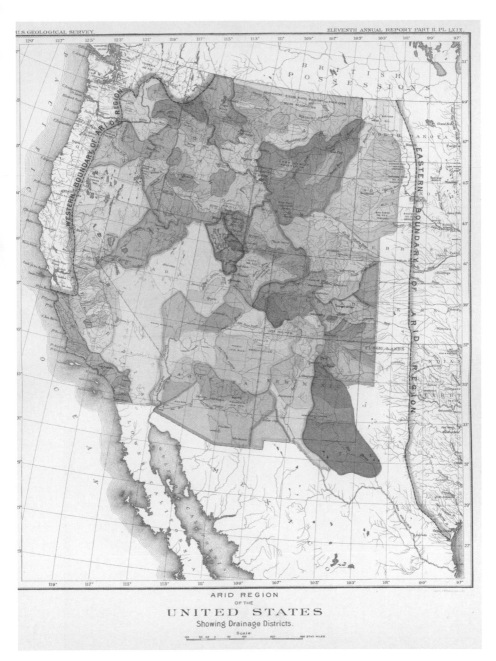

FIGURE 1. Map of watersheds of the arid West. Appears in Eleventh Annual Report of the USGS, 1889–1890. Conceived by John Wesley Powell.

FIGURE 2. William deBuys, author and historian. By Jack Loeffler.

FIGURE 3. Camillus Lopez, Tohono O'odham elder and lore-master. By Jack Loeffler.

FIGURE 4. Estevan
Arellano, author, lore-
master, *acequiero*.
By Jack Loeffler.

FIGURE 5. Gary Paul
Nabhan, poet, author,
ethnobotanist. By Jack
Loeffler.

FIGURE 6. Gary Snyder, poet, environmental philosopher.
By Jack Loeffler.

FIGURE 7. Jack Loeffler. By Katherine Loeffler.

FIGURE 8. Book signing for *Thinking Like a Watershed*, at Collected Works Bookstore, Santa Fe. Left to right: Jack Loeffler, Rina Swentzell, Estevan Arellano, Celestia Loeffler. By Seth Roffman.

FIGURE 9. Lilian Hill, Hopi environmental activist, husband Jacobo Martinez, and their twins. By Jack Loeffler.

FIGURE 10. Joe Saenz, Warm Springs Chiricahua Apache lore-master, out-fitter. By Jack Loeffler.

FIGURE 11. Lyle Balenquah, Hopi archaeologist. By Jack Loeffler.

FIGURE 12. Melissa Savage, bio-geographer, restoration ecologist. By Jack Loeffler.

FIGURE 13. Rina Swentzell, Tewa, Santa Clara, ceramicist, author. By Jack Loeffler.

FIGURE 14. Roy Kady, Navajo weaver, lore-master, sheep-herder. By Jack Loeffler.

FIGURE 15. Sarah Natani, Navajo weaver, sheep-herder. By Jack Loeffler.

FIGURE 16. Armando Torres, Seri shaman, singer, wood-carver.
By Jack Loeffler.

FIGURE 17. Stewart Udall, former US secretary of the Interior 1961–1969. By Jack Loeffler.

FIGURE 18. Shiprock, New Mexico. By Jack Loeffler.

FIGURE 19. Sunset over Indian Country. By Jack Loeffler.

FIGURE 20. Edward Abbey at a crossroads. By Jack Loeffler.

FIGURE 21. Garrett Hardin. By Jack Loeffler.

FIGURE 22. Philip Whalen. By Jack Loeffler.

FIGURE 23. Dave Foreman. By Jack Loeffler.

12. | Thinking Like a Watershed

This essay originally appeared in Green Fire Times *(November 2009).*

SEVERAL YEARS AGO, MY friend author William deBuys was writing his fine book, *Seeing Things Whole: The Essential John Wesley Powell.* He had selected several illustrations for the book including a map of the drainage areas of the arid West rendered by John Wesley Powell. This map appears in the Eleventh Annual Report of the US Geological Survey (1889–1890). Powell had wandered throughout the American West during the late nineteenth century, and recognizing that aridity was the West's primary characteristic, had organized this map of the West watershed by watershed. When Bill showed me this map, a wave of clarity rearranged my mental coordinates, and it became obvious to me that watershed thinking is key to human survival in the twenty-first century. The map is a work of art in its deepest sense. I commandeered Powell's map for the cover of my own book, *Survival Along the Continental Divide: An Anthology of Interviews.* Thanks to another friend, Craig Newbill, director of the New Mexico Humanities Council, that map is now a beautiful poster published by the council.

Powell's map is part of my daily consciousness. Powell had an evolved mind and is regarded by Bill deBuys, as well as writer, tree farmer, and environmental thinker Gary Snyder, and myself, to have been the original bioregional thinker. Here, I reiterate Snyder's articulation of what remains to me the best definition of bioregionalism: "Bioregionalism goes beyond simple geography or biology by its cultural concern, its human concern. It is to know not only the plants and animals of a place, but also the cultural information of how people live there—the ones who know how to do it. Knowing the deeper, mythic, spiritual, archetypal implications of a fir, or a coyote, or a blue jay might be to know from both inside and outside what the total implications of a place are. So it becomes a study not only of place, but a study of psyche in place. That's what makes it so interesting. In a way, it seems to me, that it's the first truly concrete step that has been taken since Kropotkin in stating how we decentralize ourselves after the second half of the twentieth century." (Snyder's entire definition of bioregionalism appears on pages 180–81 in my *Headed Upstream: Interviews with Iconoclasts* [Harbinger House: Tucson, 1989].)

If we look at Powell's map bearing in mind Gary Snyder's definition of bioregionalism, it becomes abundantly clear that there is no better way for society to organize itself than within the context of home watershed. Powell recognized that watershed boundaries make a lot more sense than our current ephemeral geopolitical boundaries. Watershed boundaries are natural boundaries that cradle biogeographical drainage systems that are inhabited by many species of biota including the human species.

Human consciousness finds deep meaning in homeland, be that meaning scientific, mythic, or eminently practical—or all of the above. Human spiritual relationship to homeland may be rooted in the territorial imperative, but that root may blossom with a consciousness so profound that it can barely be articulated. It's as though homeland, heartland and mind-land become a single entity, that a single span of human consciousness, or lifetime, is part of a whole, a whole that includes the mosaic of watersheds and seas that surround our planet, that indeed we are part of the consciousness of the planet.

Every morning at sunrise, I face east, and while watching the grasses sway in the breeze, I speak four words: "Sun, Earth, Life, Consciousness." I am grateful for the span of consciousness that is my lifetime on this beautiful, living planet Earth warmed by the Sun, adrift in space, my brief link with eternity. My four-word mantra carries me through each day, and I frequently gaze west out over that portion of the Río Grande watershed, my home watershed, to a distant peak,

Mount Taylor, that is the sacred mountain to the south for the Navajo Indians, or to the northwest to the peak of the Jemez Mountain, a super-volcano whose eastern aspect is sacred to the Tewa Indians who live in pueblos that line the banks of the Río Grande. To the north, I look into the looming reaches of the Sangre de Cristos, those Southern Rockies that form the northeastern rim of the Río Grande Watershed, and the eastern horizon of the Tewa world. All of this is visible from where I live, from where I look out over ten thousand square miles of arid, beautiful landscape that is both named and nameless, whose presence is sculpted by the passage of great epochs, and rumblings from deep within the Earth that have resulted in a mighty rift second in size only to an even greater rift in Africa. Some may regard this as a hostile environment, but to me, it is my greatest mentor and has taught me about life. To smell the aridity while headed into the wind listening to the thin, wintry whistle of a Townsend solitaire is as good as it gets.

This northern Río Grande Watershed was rendered in green by Powell, its shape vaguely resembling the profile of a seahorse as seen from the left—a seahorse dancing westward about to hop over the Continental Divide to join its sibling, the Colorado River Watershed. These two great watersheds are but modest in their yields of water. They contain the North American Southwest, and are themselves comprised of myriad smaller watersheds, each unique with its own story, its own history, its own character.

The landscape of the North American Southwest and northwestern Mexico is the most arid patch of the North American Continent. This is desert country broken by mountain ranges. The higher plateaus are frequently regarded as piñon-juniper grassland by virtue of the scattering of a few more drops of moisture than are presently received by neighboring lowland deserts. The sense of space is vast. Biota exist relative to the amount of water. Biodiversity abounds. As does cultural diversity. Aridity defines the way we biota comport ourselves. We do not belong to the verdant East. We belong to the arid West. Some of us are exotic, even within our respective species, having blown in like tumbleweeds from without, somehow affixing ourselves to this land and selecting to reestablish our sense of indigeneity. Others of us boast ancestors whose footprints were trod into this soil, then erased by the winds of antiquity.

While thinking like a mountain implies a sense of inertia, thinking like a watershed evokes a sense of constant movement, fluidity, change. The mountain contains the headwaters of the watershed and cradles biotic communities, those "sky islands" perched precariously at the top defying the possibility of extinction. Below the piedmont, the watershed fans out, expands, the water joining the main stem, thence to flow into the seas that interact with the atmosphere and begin the cyclic process anew. The interactive factors seem infinite, the metaphor too complex to be understood by a single, or even collective mind. Still, to dance about within the metaphor is comforting. Human consciousness has yet to evolve sufficiently to perceive the raw truth. It never will because consciousness evolves as the universe evolves. Consciousness is a miraculously growing dimension that responds to the ever-changing environment of the universe. Part of the trick is to differentiate between metaphor and reality and to recognize that complete understanding is beyond the purview of the human mind.

Speaking of metaphors, how about "sky islands"? The Madrean Archipelago of the American Southwest is comprised of a series of mountain ranges in Arizona and New Mexico whose peaks contain biotic communities that are separated by seas of desert. These biotic communities have migrated up mountains over a period of millennia that separates our present point in the Holocene epoch from the Pleistocene that ended over ten thousand years ago. Selected species have since evolved within these communities whose characteristics are distinct from their cousins in other sky island environments by virtue of the contiguous biotic community of yore having been sundered by the need to seek a cooler environment in which to flourish as the warming trends of the Holocene made the lower elevations uninhabitable for species accustomed to the climate of the Pleistocene. The time span has resulted in some species seeking genetic expression unique to their tiny mountaintop habitats. Their foothold is precarious. If warming trends continue, their respective biotic communities will falter by virtue of inability to migrate up into thin air.

Metaphorically, the human species is poised atop the pinnacle of a dilemma of our own making. We may not go extinct, but the environment that we've "cooked up" is burning away myriad species at a rate that parallels spasms of extinction of species that have occurred only five times throughout the previous 540 million years.

Earth's wondrous mosaic of watersheds is constantly shifting, endlessly changing. Our species, the human species, has become the dominant species, even if temporarily. Our longevity within this mosaic will be determined by our degree of wisdom and our future practices. Our wisdom must meld many components including those that may be learned only by swimming heartily within the flow of Nature.

Gradual political and economic decentralization are vital. Concurrently, we must deemphasize our sense of species self-importance, our anthropocentrism. It is unlikely that this would happen from the top down, but rather from the bottom up, literally from the grassroots. Those who have grown up in rural environments are more likely to be honed to the flow of Nature, and therefore able to align their sensibilities with the needs of homeland. Much of wisdom comes from observation and practice, from aesthetics, from trial and error, from lingering along the edges of existence rather than from a centrist position. To be able to extrapolate well involves a rarified level of consciousness. One must encompass and digest a mighty myriad of factors, realize that oneself is but a single tiny factor within that mighty myriad, then plan and react accordingly. An appropriate metaphor for that state of mind is to think like a watershed—and then proceed from watershed consciousness on behalf of the greatest good for home watershed within the entire mosaic of watersheds.

13. | The Colorado River Compact Is 100 Years Old

THE GREATER WATERSHED OF the Colorado River is a mosaic of ecosystems ranging in altitude from over 14,000 feet in the Rocky Mountains to sea level at the delta flowing into the Sea of Cortez. The river and its tributaries have carved a wondrous array of canyons including the Grand Canyon that has revealed in great detail a geologic guide through many ages to deep antiquity. The entire watershed includes a landscape of about 244,000 square miles. The Colorado River itself is about 1,440 miles long, and until the turn of the twentieth century, provided the Sea of Cortez an annual average of around fifteen million acre-feet of fresh water. An acre foot is an acre of water one foot deep and contains nearly 326,000 gallons.

For thousands of years, distant ancestors of some of today's Native American populations used the water from the river to nurture their crops. Ancestral Puebloans created irrigation systems, while farther south Indians blew seeds of edible plants into the floodplain to supplement their hunter-gatherer lifestyles. When humans first entered the ecosystem now known as the Sonoran Desert, the landscape was still a piñon-juniper grassland. Human cultures evolved as the living landscape evolved to include those humans as part of habitat.

That was before our species regarded ourselves as separate from habitat, and therefore special.

During the sixteenth century of the current era, Europeans of primarily Spanish ancestry began slowly migrating in from Mexico where they had established an extension of the Spanish Empire of yore. Then during the nineteenth century, northern Europeans and their descendants began to migrate in from the eastern portion of the North American Continent in pursuit of their presumed Manifest Destiny to claim the entirety of the continent as their own, while displacing and even slaying tens of thousands of Indigenous peoples whose ancestors had inhabited this land for well over ten thousand years.

Easterners, many of Anglo descent, entered the sunny and dry landscape of the Southwest and were appalled by the prevailing aridity with very few bodies of water that included the Río Colorado and Río Grande. As noted author Patty Limerick recounted of their perspective: "'This is the ugliest wasteland. Why would God give us this?' To then get to this next level of cognition of saying 'Oh, it's a challenge. I get it. It's put these parts together and then you'll have Ohio.'"

The Río Colorado was the southwestern river with the most water in it, and would-be agriculturalists decided to do their best to use it to develop the land for growing abundant crops. Along the western bank of the river near the present international boundary with Mexico, were great valleys that could produce every manner of flora if the land could be irrigated. Thus, they started digging a major canal into what is now the Imperial Valley of California. The resulting debacle is history. As my friend author William deBuys noted:

"At that time, geologically, the Colorado, having oscillated back and forth across its delta, had been over on the east side of the delta for a long time, and geologically it was time for it to start moving west. Well, here was the great opportunity. An open door, a heavy flow of water, and boom! It went. Essentially, the river adopted the irrigation canal as its main channel, and what then ensued was a kind of apocalyptic experience for the Imperial Valley as the river flooded and flooded and flooded with repeated storms. It followed in the spring again with snow melt, and for two years, a kind of humpty-dumpty story was played out with all the king's horses and all the king's men, trying to put the river back again. They couldn't do it for two years, until finally, with all the resources of the Southern Pacific railroad, they put together a really crack team of engineers. The gap was finally closed, and the river was constrained within its old channel."

California was developing on many levels at once. Fifty years earlier, a one-armed Civil War veteran—John Wesley Powell—selected a crew of hearty souls, and together they navigated wooden dories down through the Grand Canyon, the first humans to do so as far as is known. The canyon is rife with rapids that can swallow a boat and the humans therein in a single gulp. Somehow, they made it, and some years later made yet another boat trip through the Canyon. Powell went on to wander the arid West on horseback, unarmed as it were.

Powell thereafter became the second director of the United States Geological Survey (USGS), and the first director of the Bureau of American Ethnology (BAE). He was a brilliant man who understood more about the nature of the American West than anyone. As director of the USGS, he mapped the West watershed by watershed, and lobbied vigorously before the US Congress to organize the West politically and culturally by watersheds, with the intent that the settlers therein, learning the nature of their respective habitat, largely govern each watershed in a state of mutual cooperation. These lands would still owe fealty to the federal government, but would be somewhat decentralized, each with its respective governance compatible with their watershed habitat. The feds turned him down, eastern developers already on the move to turn the lands to the West into money. Thus, the West is divided into a hodgepodge of states largely bounded, not by natural contours and waterways in the landscape, but with state lines configured in such a way that has little to do with Nature, but everything to do with linear thinking.

The race was on, and California took an early lead, both agriculturally and population-wise. Other less developed states were greatly concerned that California would claim all the Colorado River water by establishing prior rights. Thus in 1922, representatives from seven states privy to the waters of the Colorado River watershed including Wyoming, Colorado, Utah, New Mexico, Arizona, Nevada, and California met at Bishop's Lodge near Santa Fe, New Mexico, to forge what was to become the Colorado River Compact that eventually led to the "Law of the River." The meeting was presided over by then secretary of commerce Herbert Hoover, who would later become the thirty-first president of the United States succeeding Calvin Coolidge.

The year 2022 marks the hundredth anniversary of the Colorado River Compact.

———

IN 2000, I was invited by the humanities councils of the seven states mentioned above to write grant proposals to produce a radio series as an adjunct to an existing developing project to be titled *Moving Waters: The Colorado River and the West*. I wrote and submitted proposals through the Arizona Humanities Council to both the National Endowment for the Humanities and The Ford Foundation, and was awarded funding from both organizations to proceed. Happiness was mine! By then, I'd been running rivers in the West for thirty years as well as hiking and camping throughout the Colorado Plateau and far beyond for forty years in perpetual quest of the great mystery revealed by Nature unfolding.

My old Chevy pickup with camper shell was already loaded with my camping gear. To that I added a satchel containing sound recorder, microphones, earphones, pad, pen and toothbrush, and away I went. Over the next months, I wandered throughout the watershed getting near the headwaters of the Green, Colorado, and San Juan Rivers as well as many of the communities served by the river. At that time, it was estimated that some twenty-five million humans depended on the Colorado River for at least part of if not most of their water. Today, that population is estimated to be forty million! And it is also presently revealed that there's not enough water in that system to serve both the human population and the vast irrigation districts that rely on the river for water. More on that downstream.

In preparation I read several books as well as printed research garnered by both federal and private agencies. Thus, I had some sense of the body of the "Law of the River," and I had two close friends who were Colorado River scholars. One was the aforementioned Bill deBuys whose books, *Salt Dreams* and *Seeing Things Whole: The Essential John Wesley Powell*, remain absolutely required reading. The other friend was former Arizona congressman and Secretary of the Interior Stewart Udall. I had known Stewart for over thirty years, and he provided me with insights otherwise unavailable. I have remained fortunate in my friendships through these eighty-five years of life.

Nancy Dallette, director of the overall project for the Arizona Humanities Council, provided me with names of river scholars with whom I intended to conduct recorded interviews. I didn't have a cell phone but rather a landline telephone credit card. Over the next months, I became well-acquainted with myriad public phone booths throughout seven western states. And I actually spoke with everyone on my list.

One of the most learned interviewees that I recorded was William Swan, an attorney who was an authority on the Colorado River Compact. He imparted some interesting history to me: "Congress was appropriating money for diversion works clear back in the 1800s. But when things really got rolling in the late 1800s, early 1900s, there was just simply a huge tension. Because as the West began to develop, you had the populations developing more in the Southwest, in California, and along the river in Arizona, and not so much in the other states. And the other states looking at this interstate river said, 'Whoa. Wait a minute. We may be at risk here, because under the Doctrine of Prior Appropriation, somebody who puts the water to use could claim the whole right to the river.' And so, they could eventually claim possibly all of the river flow for themselves. So, the Upper Basin states [of Wyoming, Colorado, Utah, and New Mexico] got very nervous about that, and decided to go to Congress. They asked Congress to help with the development of a compact. So, Congress consented. They appointed a referee, so to speak, in the form of Mr. [Herbert] Hoover. They sat down and tried to work out a compact. They would like, I think, to have worked out a situation where they could figure out how much each state would get. But that was just too difficult. So, they divided it into basins. The upper basin states of Wyoming, Colorado, Utah, and New Mexico, against the lower basin states of Arizona, California, and Nevada and tried to work out a division of the water, just to protect each sphere, so to speak. The upper sphere and the lower sphere. And they finally did that by thinking that the river flowed more than 15 million acre-feet a year, and divided it 50–50, 7.5 million acre-feet per year to the Upper Basin, 7.5 million to the Lower Basin, as some way of sharing the river in perpetuity so that the Upper Basin would feel secure.

"In hindsight, it is flawed because the river may not produce that much water, and they recognized at the time that Mexico would eventually need a share of that. Of course, later, in the 1940s we did work out the treaty with Mexico which gave Mexico a guaranteed million and a half [acre-feet]. When you add those up, 7.5, 7.5, and the 1.5, you are at 16.5 million acre-feet. And even the Bureau of Reclamation will say the river doesn't produce that every year. It is probably close to 15 million acre-feet, but it is not 16.5. So, we will have a crisis some day in the future. That division [Upper and Lower Basins] under the Colorado River Compact of 1922 is really the foundation of this whole thing."

The dividing line separating the Upper Basin States from the Lower Basin is located at Lee's Ferry just south of the state line between Utah and Arizona. Former Arizona Congressman and Secretary of the Interior, Stewart Udall, contends that the Colorado River Compact established in Santa Fe in 1922 led to events that enabled Californians to develop Colorado River water well in advance of the other six states:

"Herbert Hoover served them well. I have never understood why he was there. He was in effect, California's agent in putting this through. They wanted an agreement that would enable them to go to Congress and build Boulder [now Hoover] Dam. That was a kind of forced marriage. It ended up with this strange thing that never happened in other basins, of each state being allocated a certain amount of water. This is purely arbitrary. There was no rational basis for it. Hoover, I am sure, was under pressure. They had to have an agreement that led, of course, to the construction of Boulder Dam. And that enormous project went forward in the depths of the Great Depression. This again showed the political power that Southern California was exerting—and the economic power because it got the electric power companies involved. This was, in essence, a California project. It wasn't anything beneficial to the basin. And the water, other than that flowing down the river to the delta and flowing to the few irrigation districts like Imperial Valley and other huge users of water, the key water, rather good quality water was going to Southern California through an aqueduct."

California was on a roll, determined to make the most of their access to the Colorado River. They got there first and took the most. Their allocation was determined to be 4.4 million acre-feet per year, however, because the Upper Basin states were far from developing their potential of water use, California sucked up an additional 1.2 million acre-feet of unused Upper Basin water that flowed into the Lower Basin.

The water was apportioned as follows:

UPPER BASIN

Wyoming: 1.043 million acre-feet
Colorado: 3.855 million acre-feet
Utah: 1.714 million acre-feet
New Mexico: 838,000 acre-feet
Arizona: northern strip in Navajo-Hopi country—
50,000 acre-feet

LOWER BASIN

Nevada: 300,000 acre-feet
Arizona: 2.8 million acre-feet (originally 2.3 million acre-feet)
California: 4.4 million acre-feet

Arizona did not agree to their original apportionment compared to California. They didn't sign the compact, and it wasn't until forty-one years later with a Supreme Court decision in 1963 that they were annually apportioned 2.8 million acre-feet. But there was a catch. Before California would finally agree to Arizona's apportionment, Arizona had to agree to being junior to California. If there wasn't enough water for all states in the Lower Basin, Arizona would have to make up for any shortfall to California. Stewart Udall elucidates: "The Santa Fe [Colorado River] Compact simply divided waters and produced interstate agreements, although Arizona refused to participate. And they fought it for twenty years because they saw it as California as getting the upper hand and dominating the river. They were correct, in my opinion, in that assumption. But they had to have a law and that became the Boulder Canyon Project, which would spell out what was going to happen if this big dam was built. That was the beginning, really, of what they now call the 'Law of the River.' This was a lawyer's dream. Lawyers in all the affected states had to become acquainted with the law, and then additional laws were written. And now there is a body of law called 'The Law of the River.' This is not true in any other river basin in the United States to this degree. Law governs everything."

Many people who analyze the relative strengths of different states think that California had the most influence and therefore got the best deal with the 1922 compact. Floyd Dominy served as commissioner for the Bureau of Reclamation overseeing the critical period of dam building in the mid-twentieth century. He disagrees: "As a matter of fact, I am kind of surprised that the compact doesn't favor California more than it does. When you stop and think that the time that compact was drafted, in the 1920s, there were fifteen congressmen from California and Arizona and Nevada. There were only eight in the Upper Basin states. So, the population already favored California. And the influence in Congress already favored California. I'm kind of surprised that it came out the way it did. Now, the reason it did was because California wanted Hoover Dam. And they wanted the

All-American Canal. They had to have some support from the rest of the West in order to get that. I think, actually, it turned out quite favorably for the Upper Basin states."

In Santa Barbara, I interviewed Norris Hundley, author of *The Great Thirst*, and most insightful lifelong Colorado River scholar, who spoke of other inadequacies of 1922 Colorado River Compact: "An important thing to keep in mind about the compact is that it reflects its time in being an ethnocentric document. The Indians weren't invited to participate, nor was there any consideration of giving them a share of the water. Hoover said, 'We don't want to put a wild Indian provision in here, create a problem for ourselves.' Mexico asked to have representation. Prior to this time, it would go on for another two decades. Mexico had been negotiating with the United States over rights to Colorado River water and to water in the Río Grande. The compact negotiator said 'No' to inviting Mexicans. 'We don't want to have the Mexicans here.' Everyone suspected there would someday be a treaty. The basins would share that Mexican burden as they called it. But other than that, nothing was said."

I would add that this was also an anthropocentric document in that it served only presumed human needs. It took absolutely no consideration for the myriad other species of biota that abounded, including fish, reptiles, mammals, birds, plant-life—or even the geophysical damage wrought by construction of dams and waterways that now crisscross the fragile desert habitats of the North American Southwest. The document was also Anglo-centric, written in English, prompted by the long cultural history of hegemony that characterized the prevailing political hierarchy that continues to this day.

Thus it was that the enormous Boulder [now Hoover] Dam was constructed. It took a number of years, much of the construction occurring during the Great Depression that began in 1929 when the stock market crashed. California was also able to construct the All-American Canal beginning in 1934 that extends from the river westward for about eighty-two miles just north of the international boundary between California and Mexico. Its waters irrigate over a half-million acres of the Imperial Valley that provides an enormous amount of produce and revenue.

It took American involvement in World War II to result in a water treaty with Mexico.

Stewart Udall: "The history of the 1944 treaty with Mexico was during the war, 1944, and obviously was an effort by President Roosevelt to mollify the Mexican officials. They had agriculture south of the Imperial Valley. And Baja, California was a rich agricultural area, and they wanted to protect their water. And they said, 'You divided up the river, but you left us out.' And so, this treaty guaranteed Mexico a certain amount of water. And that was the 1944 US–Mexico Treaty. It wasn't a treaty with the states. It was the United States of America and the government of Mexico."

Stewart also told me that he thought that President Roosevelt made that treaty happen to ensure that Mexico wouldn't allow Axis forces to set up military bases in Mexico to result in bringing World War II to American soil.

With Boulder Dam and the All-American Canal, California was in the catbird seat. They were using every drop of their allotted 4.4 million acre-feet from the Colorado River. However, California needed even more water to serve major cities including Los Angeles, Santa Monica, and Santa Ana. Thus, yet another aqueduct was planned. But first, another dam must be constructed, hence the Parker Dam was designed and built and resulted in another reservoir known as Lake Havasu. That dam was completed in 1935, and the Colorado River Aqueduct started transporting water from the Colorado River to the great cities to the west.

Arizona politicians seethed at what they regarded as grave injustice. If California was to get their great water project, Arizonans wanted their project as well. Arizona took their complaint to the Supreme Court. Decisions were delayed for eleven more years thanks to California politicians. But finally, in 1963, the Supreme Court decided in favor of Arizona by awarding them 2.8 million acre-feet plus the instate flow of the Gila River that originates near Silver City, New Mexico. Its tributaries include the Salt and Verde Rivers.

There was a catch. In order to secure California's votes of approval, Arizona had to agree that under no circumstances could California be deprived of its allotted 4.4 million acre-feet unless the river ran so low that there wasn't that much water flowing into the Lower Basin. Indeed, Arizona agreed, but it would take a century before Arizona had to reduce its allotment. More on that downstream.

Arizona had long dreamt of its own project. The dream project known as the Central Arizona Project (CAP) was born. Earlier on in 1902, the Reclamation Act had been passed, resulting in the US Reclamation Service (now Bureau of Reclamation) whose main purpose was to serve agriculturalists by providing water for irrigation. Thus, by 1911, the Salt River had been dammed to provide irrigation waters to farmers in southern Arizona. The dam, now called Roosevelt Dam after Theodore, was also capable of providing hydroelectricity. The entire project was deemed a great success and became known as the Salt River Project.

The Central Arizona Project was to be modeled after the Salt River Project. The plan was to pump water from Lake Havasu from a pumping station situated on the east bank that would pump water up and over mountain ranges in a lined ditch to supply irrigation water to farmers in the central valleys of Arizona. This would require electricity. The plan was to construct yet two more dams on the Colorado River, the Bridge Canyon Dam just south of Grand Canyon and the Marble Canyon Dam just north of Grand Canyon. These would be "cash register dams" whose sole purpose was to generate electricity to run the pumping station on Lake Havasu to pump water into central Arizona.

At which point, David Brower, one of the greatest environmentalists of the twentieth century, stepped into the breech and said, "NO WAY!" as only Dave could. Earlier on, partnering with Martin Litton, with the support of the Sierra Club they had thwarted construction of the proposed Echo Park and Split Mountain Dams to have been constructed near the confluence of the Green and Yampa Rivers that would have resulted in a reservoir that would have flooded part of Dinosaur National Monument.

Martin Litton was a great adventurer who had wooden dories constructed after the same design used by John Wesley Powell nearly a century earlier. Litton was also a photographer and journalist who learned of the proposed Echo Park Dam and headed north to document it for the *Los Angeles Times*. I interviewed Martin Litton in his home in 2001. He had this to say: "I got a call from David Brower, whom I didn't know, but I think I had heard of him. It was 1952. That is when he became executive director of the Sierra Club. And he had heard of me because he had seen these articles in the Los Angeles Times I had been running, which were pretty rabid. They were pro-natural environment, and nothing else. He wanted me to come and join him in doing great things with the Sierra Club. He was on fire. And we decided to get together and work together on this within the Sierra Club in stopping the Split Mountain and Echo Park Dams in Dinosaur National Monument. The Sierra Club achieved its first real conservation victory in those four years. We sit back, and I am very much a part of it by then, and say, 'My God, how did that happen? We saved Dinosaur.' In saving Dinosaur, you are not just talking about a quarry with dinosaur bones in it. You are talking about a vast magnificent area that is worthy of the same kind of attention as any other National Park. There is a symbolism to it."

Floyd Dominy was commissioner of the Bureau of Reclamation in the mid-twentieth century. He was born in 1913 and grew up on a dry farm in Nebraska during the Dust Bowl years. He was relentless in his pursuit of greening-up the landscape of the arid West by building dams to provide water for countless irrigation projects and to generate hydroelectricity for both pumping water and to power the cities of the West. "A lot of people get confused. They think that Echo Park was a substitute for Glen Canyon or that Glen Canyon was a substitute for Echo Park. Actually, Glen Canyon Dam would have been needed whether or not Echo Park and Split Mountain were authorized. They were strictly "cash register" dams that were on the Green River. They didn't provide the huge carry-over storage that was required that Glen Canyon would do. Now, it is said that it is just a matter of poor nomenclature that they got defeated. If they would have been called Rattlesnake Butte and Snake Hollow, we could have got them authorized. But to talk about Echo Park and Split Mountain, it was a bad nomenclature. At any rate, Dave Brower and company had beat the bureau hands down on that one."

What was that about Glen Canyon Dam? This dam and resulting Lake Powell Reservoir was Floyd Dominy's dream dam. In 1956, the Colorado River Storage Project (CRSP) went into effect in order to provide water storage upstream from Lee's Ferry so that the Upper Basin would be able to guarantee 8.3 million acre-feet of water to the Lower Basin during the dry years. I interviewed Rick Gold, an authority on the subject in Salt Lake City.

"The Colorado River Storage Project yielded a plan for a storage project that is actually an amalgam of several mainstream units, as they are called, Glen Canyon [Dam] being one of those. Aspinall Unit being another, and three dams over in Colorado that include the Navajo Unit [Dam], and the Flaming Gorge Unit [Dam]. Those [dams] are called the mainstream, or the initial, units of the Colorado River Storage Project. [There are] about twenty-one other associated projects called the "participating" projects. And those projects are called participators because they participate through the funding mechanism of power revenues, helping to repay the irrigation aid for irrigation in the Upper Basin. Those mainstream units, all except Navajo [Dam] in CRSP have federal hydropower. And that hydropower generates power at cost . . . and is sold to the public power utilities across the West. The revenue that comes from the sale of that hydro-power generation then not only pays for the investment in hydropower, but it pays for that portion of the irrigation investment that is beyond the individual irrigator's ability to repay [hence the term "cash register dams"]. And that is sort of the background of what and why the Colorado River Storage Project came into being. It was an Upper Basin-wide plan for the development of the

Colorado River, through storage, initial units, and through participating projects."

Thus, in 1956, construction began on the most contested dam in America—the Glen Canyon Dam. Shortly thereafter, a student at the University of New Mexico named Edward Abbey and his buddy, Ralph Newcomb, decided to go adventuring in Glen Canyon. They borrowed a couple of old rafts, tied them together, and away they went through one of the most beautiful canyons in the world. Then near the end of their trip, they encountered the construction of the dam that would flood Glen Canyon, drown it, bury it beneath yet another reservoir on the Colorado River second in size only to Lake Mead formed by the Hoover Dam downstream. To say that they were monumentally pissed off is an understatement. Abbey, who was a burgeoning author, wrote eloquently about this debacle in his classic book of essays, *Desert Solitaire*. In my opinion, it was this extraordinary book that invigorated the genesis of the radical environmental movement after its publication in 1968 when many of America's youth were engaging in what came to be known as the counterculture movement.

But back to the subject at hand, when Dave Brower and the Sierra Club thoroughly thwarted the Bureau of Reclamation's scheme to construct dams at either end of the Grand Canyon, proclaiming that the bureau was going to flood Grand Canyon! Another source of electricity had to be found. If dams weren't the answer, what next? There was known to be an abundant coal deposit in northern Arizona buried in Black Mesa. It was located in Indian Country—Hopi and Navajo country, and a landform deeply sacred to both cultures. The answer was simple. Build a coal-fired electrical generating station using coal from Black Mesa and send the electricity south to the pumping station on the eastern bank of Lake Havasu.

Floyd Dominy: "The Bureau [of Reclamation] had been studying these means of supplying that water out of the Colorado River into Central Arizona. Then we had determined that the water could be pumped out of Lake Havasu and carried across the country in lined canals, reaching Phoenix and Tucson. Of course, we recognized that this is a very expensive project.

"The compromise to building Bridge Canyon Dam was to build a huge coal-fired plant, partly underwritten by the federal government and the rest of it by the Salt River Project and other power users. Power developers. The pumping power to pump the water for the Central Arizona Project comes from this coal-fired plant. You can visualize a plant that burns a trainload of coal a day—that is how big it is. Two and a half million-kilowatt-capacity. The government invested in that proposal in order to have power for the Central Arizona Project."

The power plant was constructed on the shores of Lake Powell near Page, Arizona. The coal was to be strip-mined from Black Mesa and transported via a specially constructed railroad extending from the north end of Black Mesa to the power plant at Lake Powell. The power plant was to become known as the Navajo Generating Station, and about 25 percent of the electricity generated there was to be used to power up the Central Arizona Project. This was yet another tidy political package dreamed up to foster growth for the sake of growth.

I'd caught wind of a proposed strip mine some years earlier when I was spending a fair amount of time on the Navajo Reservation working on different projects. But it wasn't until 1969 when a stout-hearted Park Service historian by the name of William Brown told me what he had come to learn through scuttlebutt leaked from the Department of the Interior. Bill told me about the proposed strip mine, the coal-fired power plant, AND that water was to be pumped from the Pleistocene aquifer beneath Black Mesa to slurry coal to yet another existing power plant near Laughlin, Nevada.

Bill and I hopped in my old black Chevy carryall and headed out to Black Mesa. We drove the length of a bumpy, two-track dirt road from the north end to the south end of Black Mesa and saw where the intended strip mine was to be located. Thereafter, we rented a motor boat at Lee's Ferry on the Colorado River and putted about eighteen miles upstream through what little remained of Glen Canyon until we rounded a bend and looked up into the face of the Glen Canyon Dam, the monster that stoppered the river—the flow of Nature through the North American Southwest. We were speechless. We were witness to that which symbolized the entry of the Southwest into what became known as the "National Sacrifice Area." The magnitude of what was to ensue was beyond imagination.

Shortly thereafter, I went to visit an elderly Hopi friend whom I had known for some years. His name was David Monongye, and he lived in Hotevilla on Third Mesa. I told David what I had learned so far. He asked to me to stay until the following day. He contacted many other traditional Hopis, and the next day, we all met on Second Mesa. David introduced me and asked me to recount what I had told him the previous day. Thus, I repeated the dreary news that a coal strip mine had been scheduled for Black Mesa and that water was to be extracted at the rate of 2,000 gallons a minute to slurry coal 273 miles to the west to an existing power plant and that a railroad was to be constructed to haul coal across the Kaibito Plateau that extended between Black Mesa and Page, Arizona. I told them that this was under contract between their Hopi Tribal Council chaired by Clarence Hamilton and the Peabody Coal Co. of East St. Louis with the blessing of the federal government. All sixty-three Hopis rose as a single body, each of them enraged, especially at their tribal council for selling out a sacred landform. For a few minutes, I thought violence might ensue—but it didn't. They calmed down, and David introduced me to Thomas Banyacya who spoke fair English. There was discussion and Thomas turned to me and asked me on behalf of the traditional Hopis if I would help them get the message to the American public about the nature of this travesty. I agreed, and some days later back in Santa Fe, Bill Brown, Jim Hopper, and I founded the Black Mesa Defense Fund. Soon we were joined by Terry Moore, and thereafter, by Tom Andrews.

For three years, we did our level best to halt the "rape of Black Mesa." But we'd taken on the Central Arizona Project. We had brought the plight of the Hopis before the eyes of the American public. We vigorously fought coal-fired power plants in general. We were later called "radical environmentalists" and even "ecoterrorists." The truth is we were fighting federal and corporate ecoterrorism full tilt. Three years later when we realized that we were exhausted and in debt, we admitted that we'd lost that battle. But before we finally closed the doors on the Black Mesa Defense Fund, we paid off every cent of debt and left as honorably as we could.

Only much later would I understand that the Law of the River was responsible for the Central Arizona Project, the construction of the Glen Canyon Dam and the flooding of Glen Canyon, and extreme population growth in the most arid part of North America. As Ed Abbey once said to me as we looked down on the Sonoran Desert from near our campsite in the Superstition Mountains, "The Central Arizona Project has led to the metastasis of Phoenix and Tucson."

The Central Arizona Project cost about four billion dollars, far more than originally anticipated. The Colorado River water pumped so many miles from Lake Havasu to Phoenix and Tucson was too expensive for most farmers. Thus, many of them sold their land to developers, and now vast spans of the beautiful, luxuriant, and fragile Sonoran Desert have been turned into money lining corporate and political pockets.

Dave Brower, by then head of Friends of the Earth, and I had become friends. At one point, we were part of a group of hikers who hiked down Coyote Gulch to the confluence with the Río Escalante. Beforehand, we spent time at different southwestern strip mines staring into the devastation. At one point, we were invited to an escorted (guarded) tour through part of the Four Corners Power Plant near Shiprock.

Thereafter, we camped together near the base of the mighty Shiprock in northwestern New Mexico that Dave had climbed in 1939 when he was twenty-seven years old. I interviewed Dave for a radio series I produced in 1986.

David Brower: "I kept learning. I first thought that you could save a lot of rivers by going to nuclear power. Then I found that was no good. So I was willing to save rivers by going to coal, and found that was no good. And I finally smartened up and found out the way to save rivers and coal and avoid nuclear power is to take a whole new look at our ideas about economic growth, and to ask the essential questions: 'What kind of economic growth must we have? And what kind can we, and the Earth, no longer afford?' And that is where my thinking has been ever since the Colorado River Project."

The Peabody Coal Company created a huge strip mine that devastated much of Black Mesa. In so doing, it also wrought enormous damage to both Hopi and Navajo traditional cultures by eradicating systems of values based on living in harmony with Nature and gravely endangering a level of Indigenous mindedness without which our human species may not survive. And that has been the focus of much of my own work ever since the rape of Black Mesa.

––––––––

THE *Moving Waters* radio series was produced in 2001 and included everything mentioned above and far more. Twenty-one years have since passed since that series premiered. The good news is that the Navajo Generating Station is no more. The enormous smokestacks that had spewed thousands of tons of ruinous pollutants into the once pellucid air of the North American Southwest were lawfully blown to smithereens with explosives on February 11, 2021, a sight that brought tears of joy to many of us who bear enduring love for this Earth. Terry Moore, Black Mesa Defense Fund stalwart, and author/adventurer Morgan Sjogren both sent me contrasting video clips of the event. I thought of Ed Abbey who would have cheered vigorously at the sight. I hope that his bones were able to spin in celebration in his hidden grave.

Now, one hundred years after the signing of the Colorado River Compact, Nature's principles are visibly thwarting federal legislation. Global warming and climate instability have resulted in an enduring drought in the North American Southwest (the most severe in 1,200 years). The bottom line here is that there is not enough precipitation to meet the legislated annual quota of 16.5 million acre-feet to serve both the Upper and Lower Basins and Mexico, and there hasn't been for several years. Both Lakes Mead and Powell have shrunk considerably. Lake Powell has a bathtub ring almost a hundred feet high, and Lake Mead is less than half-full. If the drought continues as predicted, the watershed will release less water into the Colorado River, and the two great reservoirs will continue to diminish, especially if both Upper and Lower Basins insist on taking their shares allocated a hundred years ago. There is a point known as dead pool when the water is too low to even turn the turbines that generate a significant proportion of electricity throughout the West. So far, that is not the case.

Legislators have been engaged in discussions to determine the feasibility of revised legislation. There has been talk of decommissioning the Glen Canyon Dam so that the entire flow of the river would drain into Lake Mead. Upper Basin states are adamantly opposed to decommissioning Glen Canyon Dam because that would inevitably deprive those states from developing as they would with a guarantee of 7.5 million acre-feet to split up. Already, agricultural and urban water users are vying for the water, especially in the region of Imperial Valley and southern Arizona. The complexity in economics is a fundamental issue.

Twenty years ago, the Colorado River served twenty-five million humans. Presently it serves forty million humans. As human population increases, precipitation decreases due largely to climate change brought on by many factors including too much CO_2 in the atmosphere, a fair proportion of which emanated from the great coal-fired electrical generating stations including the now defunct Navajo Generating Station.

In 2022 for the first time, Arizona will have to relinquish 500,000 acre-feet of its allocation so that California can take its apportioned share, Arizona being junior to California as determined in the Law of the River. Inter-basin transfers of water have also come into effect. For example, the San Juan-Chama Diversion that normally diverts 110,000 acre-feet of water through a twenty-three-mile-long tunnel carved beneath the Continental Divide extending from the greater Colorado River Watershed into the Chama River, a major tributary of the Río Grande, puts Albuquerque in direct competition with Los Angeles, San Diego, Phoenix, and Tucson for Colorado River water. As New Mexico water attorney, scholar, and author Em Hall so aptly pointed out in a recorded interview I conducted in 2010, "Albuquerque essentially has thrown itself into a common pot with Las Vegas, Phoenix, Tucson, and Los Angeles. Guess how they're going to do when push comes to shove in that kind of world?"

At the same time, the Navajo Indians want to run a pipeline from Lake Powell inland to supplement their limited groundwater. Indians have prior water rights according to the Winter's Doctrine of 1908. Never forget that for many years, the Peabody Coal Co. tapped the Navajo aquifer to the tune of two thousand gallons a minute in order to slurry coal from Black Mesa strip mine to the Mohave Generating station near Laughlin, Nevada, to generate electricity to light up Las Vegas and other areas.

The citizens of Utah want to run a pipeline westward to St. George to provide that growing city with Colorado River water. The citizens of the Las Vegas area have created a deep pipeline from the bottom of Lake Mead to suck out the last drops of water when Mead runs dry. The common pot grows larger as water diminishes here in the Southwest.

Some traditional Indians continue to conceive of providing healthy habitat for their descendants seven generations hence. Healthy habitat includes all of the species—not just the human species—who live there.

Presently, over 80 percent of the human population of the United States lives in urban environments. Others of us live in more rural environments. This must affect our perspective very deeply. We who live in rural habitats are aware of the wildlife, the diversity of flora and fauna that occur here naturally, especially if we allow our consciousness to extend beyond our personal agendas. Traditional Indigenous peoples whose perspectives have not been subsumed by monoculture have a much broader view of the flow of Nature than most of the rest of us.

Sarah Natani is a Navajo weaver who has herded her sheep for many years near Table Mesa south of Shiprock, New Mexico. She recalls drinking water from the San Juan River during her younger days:

"Well, my uncle, his name was Ben D'datin, and he had a farm over there. There was a big ditch over there where they used to pump the water through there. We got a bucket and drank that water, and none of us ever got sick from drinking that San Juan River. And I know that water is very precious to everybody, not only Navajos or white men or anybody. The Great Spirit has put the water there for us, to all share it, to use it. Not one person takes over the whole water."

Vernon Masayesva is an educator and former tribal chairman for his Hopi people. For decades, he has assiduously pursued protecting the waters both within and on the surface of his homeland.

"I go to these meetings when they talk about the Colorado River. And they talk about the Law of the River and how all these people have an economic interest in it. They have a vested interest. They all look at the river as theirs. It is my river. That is the mentality. That is the mind-set. It is there for me to use. To exploit. To make more money. And I don't want you taking it away from me. So they fight to keep it. It is their water. They forget that the river does not belong to us. That we belong to it. We don't control the river. We think we do. We write laws about it. And it gives us a sense of ownership and control. It controls us. The river controls us. But we don't look at it like that. My hope is that we would change that some way. And I think there is a way to still benefit from the river, to bring the health back to the river. We have taken so much of it. We have got to give something back. That is the Hopi way. Whatever you take, you always give back. You never just take, take, take. You don't say, 'I am separate from the plant or the animal or the stars.' That is why in many of our kachina dances, when we participate with our 'friends' as we call them, we become those things. We have no problem with it. One day I am the moon. The next day I am the badger. I would transform into those things. And it just reinforces the feeling that we are in this interconnection here. We are not separate from Nature. We are all an integral part of it."

———

HEGEMONY, OLIGARCHY, PLUTOCRACY—the prevailing aristocracy that has long dominated so much of human cultural perspective through the millennia. Yet to me, the only true aristocracy is one of consciousness.

In consciousness we trust . . .

14. | On Direct Action

This essay originally appeared in Earth Island Journal *(May 23, 2022).*

IN A RECENT *New Scientist* magazine, Swedish professor of ecology Andreas Malm was interviewed about his thoughts concerning waging battle on behalf of the environment in view of the corporate hierarchy's chilly—and often obstructionist—response to calls for action on climate change. The title of his latest book, *How to Blow Up a Pipeline: Learning to Fight in a World on Fire*, in which he makes the case for moving beyond peaceful protest in order to spur climate action, invigorated an immediate reaction in my own mind. Over fifty years ago, a tiny coterie of us were doing our best to forestall continued construction of coal-fired power plants in the North American Southwest. Concurrently I found myself contemplating sabotage of a pipeline.

Because of the legal shenanigans of a Utah-based lawyer named John Boyden, Peabody Coal constructed a pipeline that ran 273 miles from an enormous strip mine located on Black Mesa in northern Arizona to the Mohave Generating Station near Laughlin, Nevada. Water was to be pumped from the pristine Pleistocene aquifer beneath Black Mesa at two thousand gallons per minute and used to slurry crushed coal through the pipeline to the power plant. Boyden had negotiated a contract between the Hopi Tribal Council that had hired him, and the Peabody Coal Co. of East Saint Louis for whom he worked on the sly. He received at least a million dollars for serving two disparate entities.

The Black Mesa mine was situated on a landform that remains deeply sacred to both traditional Hopi and Navajo Indians. The water from the aquifer feeds springs in the Hopi villages and also wells that provide water to Navajo Indians living in the region around Black Mesa, desert country by any standard. In other words, this was an environmental debacle of magnitude. Coal was to be strip-mined from a sacred landform, and water was to be sucked from a life-sustaining aquifer. To complete the fiasco, more coal would be shipped on a new railroad from the strip mine to the enormous Navajo Generating Station under construction on the shores of Lake Powell, which straddles Utah and Arizona. The Mohave and Lake Powell power plants would contribute to an already burgeoning amount of carbon dioxide, sulfur, and nitrous oxides, and particulate matter into the atmosphere. On top of that, power lines were to be constructed across one of the most beautiful landscapes in America. About 25 percent of the electricity generated by the new Navajo Generating Station was to be used to pump water from the Colorado River through a concrete-lined ditch into the Central Valleys of Arizona, ostensibly to serve agriculturalists. In the end, the water was used primarily by developers to result in the metastasis of both Phoenix and Tucson as they spread across the fragile landscape of the Sonoran Desert.

This entire undertaking, the Central Arizona Project (CAP), ultimately involved every element of environmental devastation, not the least of which was irreparable damage to two Native American cultures through total disregard for their traditional perspectives.

Back when the project was still under development, I traveled along many miles of that coal-slurry pipeline considering wreaking some form of explosive mayhem to shut it down. I thought about it but didn't do it. Why? Because I realized that I'd certainly get caught and end up in prison for many years, and that wasn't where I wanted to spend my life. At least that was part of my reasoning. Another was that I detest violence, even against inanimate objects like a pipeline. Also, the thought of possibly causing harm to a fellow human is abhorrent to me. I imagined electricity suddenly going off in a hospital in Las Vegas causing death on operating tables. Thus, I abandoned any notion of blowing up that pipeline or any others.

I have to say that I was not alone all those years ago in trying to defend habitat against invasion by corporate extractors. My friend Edward Abbey started his defense of habitat earlier than I, but he was nine years older. Another who comes to mind is the late great Dave Brower, who helped us considerably as we fought to save the Southwest from coal-fired power plants. In 1972, Dave and I were invited to visit the Four Corners Power Plant near Shiprock in northwestern New Mexico. Shortly after we were led into the computer room wherein monstrous computers tended to the digitized operation of the power plant, Dave turned to me and said loudly, "Hey Loeffler—did you bring the satchel charge?" He was goading our guides, of course, and we were immediately escorted off of the premises. (Dave Brower would later go on to found Earth Island Institute.)

———

THE AFOREMENTIONED ANDREAS MALM advocates sabotage in defense against climate change. I haven't read his book and chances are good that I won't. Malm has apparently spiced up his Marxist leanings by including an environmental imperative.

While I don't necessarily agree with him, I understand the instinct. Some decades ago, someone coined the term "ecotage," which means to commit sabotage for ecological reasons. Thereafter, the term "ecoterrorism" was erroneously defined as the practice of committing sabotage to thwart environmental damage committed by extractors of natural resources. When I consider ecoterrorism, I immediately think of the true ecoterrorists, namely extractors, developers, and their men and women in government who are invigorating mayhem against the natural environment. They are terrorizing habitat and its inhabitants. However, those who defend habitat are the ones who get arrested while those who destroy it are often protected by legislation—legislation that disregards the laws and principles of Nature. Whose laws do you abide by? Or I abide by?

Each of us has to define and attend to our personal ethical

standards. As Ed Abbey said, "Freedom begins between the ears." I deeply admire Mahatma Gandhi who greatly inspired nonviolent civil disobedience—and who was assassinated for his efforts the year I turned twelve years old. I also greatly admire the many Native Americans who recently defended sacred land against yet another pipeline at Standing Rock, also peacefully. My heart went out to them, and I laud their courage and persistence. They stood it down and did not use violence. They practiced civil disobedience in the face of legislation that runs counter to Nature's principles, and they won.

Here we are on this tiny planet Earth, less than eight thousand miles in diameter, which, in partnership with the Sun, spawned us and every other form of life that has ever lived here over the last 3.8 billion years or so. And with life came cognition and now consciousness. We may not be the only truly conscious species, but we're the only one that has gravely misused this fantastic gift of consciousness. It's never too late for any of us to use our consciousness with imagination and enthusiasm to become activists on behalf of Earth. If enough of us get into the act, we can turn around the death-spawn of our own invention.

However you choose to turn it around, JUST DO IT.

15. | A Case for Naturist Anarchism

This essay originally appeared in Green Fire Times *(February 2018).*

ANARCHISM IN ITS HIGHEST sense requires the practice of individual self-discipline and self-governance within both societal and ecological contexts. According to Edward Abbey, pure anarchism and pure democracy amount to the same thing: "The problem of democracy is the problem of power—how to keep power decentralized, equally distributed, fairly shared. Anarchism means maximum democracy: the maximum possible dispersal of political power, economic power, and force—military power. The anarchist society consists of a voluntary association of self-reliant, self-supporting autonomous communities."

Naturism, on the other hand, is deep recognition of one's place in Nature both intellectually and intuitively wherein one fully comprehends one's sense of kindredness with all fellow organisms as well as the perception of one's respective habitat as a self-regenerating, living cognitive system. Thus naturist anarchism is a culture of practice founded on collective consciousness of being part of the flow of Nature within one's home ecosystem and that we are governed first and foremost by the needs of the ecosystem/watershed/bioregion to which we are secondary, even though we appear to be the dominant species. Put another way, our culture of practice is to be determined by consensus from within a biocentric system of ethics rather than the anthropocentric/economic context to which we are presently culturally accustomed. This takes anarchism to an entirely new level that addresses not only human egalitarianism, but also complete recognition of the natural needs of homeland. In this sense, homeland metaphorically sits at the head of the table of any self-governing body.

Enormous obstacles to overcome include our anthropocentric attitudes and our centralized governance, currently dominated by economic rather that ecological principles. Unless human cultural attitudes and practices are brought into alignment with Nature's principles, rather than driven by oligarchic enclaves, we approach the end of our tenure as a highly manipulative dominant species. Our monoculture of practice is at odds with a naturist perspective. However, many of our Indigenous cultures indeed embody naturist perspective. Profound examples may be found in many of the Indian pueblos that line the banks of the Río Grande like gardens of consciousness. We must hearken to their "Indigenous mindedness" rather than continue to subsume them. They are seedpods of human survival potential in an age of extinction of species wrought by human overpopulation, expenditure of finite resources, and attendant destruction of habitat—the natural environment of the planetary biotic community.

In America today, less than 20 percent of our human population live in rural areas while over 80 percent live in urban areas. This verifies for me that our cultural perspective is shaped largely by urban lifestyles and may thereby be regarded as supremely anthropocentric. And very few if any of us is free of some level of digital engagement in virtual reality shaped by human imagination. Thus, we are dominated by myriad relics of human provenance including cultural mores, religious beliefs, systems of governance, public and private education, global economics—institutionalized imperatives of every order.

Our sense of the biocentric is rapidly waning within the commons of human consciousness.

In 1842, Peter Kropotkin was born into the Russian nobility and later served as an officer in the Russian Army. He withdrew from the gentry and gradually become a world-class naturalist. He was deeply influenced by the writing of Charles Darwin and undertook to write vigorously about the role of mutual aid in the evolution of species. On page 300 in his magnum opus, *Mutual Aid: A Factor of Evolution*, he writes: "In the practice of mutual aid, which we can retrace to the earliest beginnings of evolution, we thus find the positive and undoubted origin of our ethical conceptions; and we can confirm that in the ethical progress of man, mutual support—not mutual struggle—has had the leading part. "

In my opinion, Peter Kropotkin was a profoundly intelligent anarchist naturist philosopher whose influence extends into the present. Kropotkin's anarchism occurred in part as a response to the presence of the Industrial Revolution that rendered many human handcrafted lifestyles obsolete. He wanted to elevate the living standards of the peasant classes who were held in sway by the gentry. He despised the hardcore centralized bureaucratized form of governance espoused by the brand of communism that came to prevail in post-revolution Russia. He realized that centralized governance inevitably results in oligarchy that must be resisted wholeheartedly. By virtue of his beliefs and practices, he was forced to live in exile for over half his life. He believed that his fellow humans could muster the discipline to govern themselves appropriately and well. He regarded revolution as a hastening of the process of cultural evolution. But he qualified his revolutionary perspective by stating: "No struggle can be successful if it does not render itself a clear and concise account of its aim."

He made his aim quite clear in his own definition of an anarchist society that I noted earlier in this book and reiterate here: "The anarchists conceive a society in which all its members are regulated, not by laws, not by authorities, whether self-imposed or elected, but by mutual agreements between the members of that society, and by a sum of social customs and habits—not petrified by law, routine or superstition, but concordance with the ever-growing requirements of a free life, stimulated by the progress of science, invention, and the steady growth of higher ideals. No ruling authorities, then. No government of man by man; no crystallization and immobility, but a continual evolution—such as we see in Nature."

The first edition of *Mutual Aid* was published in 1902 when the human population of the planet numbered around 1.6 billion. Today, we're upward of 7.9 billion, a 475 percent increase that is now creating enormous stress on the overall planetary ecosystem. Indeed, acute stress carves the countenances of scores of millions of fellow humans who struggle desperately to survive starvation, lack of potable water, suitable shelter, grievous sanitation conditions, and war. Mutual aid is waning in America and elsewhere, especially over the last years. From early 2017 till early 2021, America was governed by a goety of oligarchs presided over by a narcissistic demagogue who continues to foreshorten future human history. The American experiment in democracy is gravely threatened by virtue of corporate economics, centralized governance, gerrymandering, greed, lust for power, and attendant spiritual malaise.

In the late nineteenth century, while Peter Kropotkin struggled to promulgate his anarchist vision in Europe and beyond, a one-armed Civil War veteran named John Wesley Powell plead his case before the Congress of the United States to organize the arid lands west of the hundredth meridian watershed by watershed, thence to be governed mainly by the residents who lived therein. Congress shot him down, unwilling to give western watershed citizens the authority of even partial self-governance and firmly established the arbitrary geopolitical boundaries that actually remain throughout the West to this day. Entrepreneurs were already on the march determined to reap the rewards of Manifest Destiny.

In all likelihood, neither Kropotkin nor Powell envisioned the imminent population explosion both here and everywhere that utterly rearranged the relationship of humankind to habitat. The demographic shift from rural countryside to urban concrete canyons has resulted in our journey down the "anthropo-scenic" highway, a highway that is largely heedless of its debilitating encroachment into every habitat through which it passes. We have woven a system of cultural attitudes that is out of phase with a biocentric ethical imperative that demands ecological balance. The lethal specter of climate instability and climate change fails to hold public attention, let alone the failing attention of many politicians in our country.

Perhaps it's appropriate to hearken to Ed Abbey's provocative apothegm: "A patriot must always be ready to defend his country against his government."

Just how can that be done? Many years ago, Ed Abbey and I knelt on the bridge that spans the Colorado River just downstream from the Glen Canyon Dam. We prayed for an earthquake and chanted in the hope that our prayers and incantations would result in a mighty geophysical shiver that would shake that dam loose and release the unnaturally impounded waters. Nary a quiver, thus we concluded that it would take more than our prayers to return the landscape to its natural state.

What about eco-guerilla warfare? For me, the notion of inflicting bodily harm on any fellow human—except in self-defense and defense of family—is fundamentally wrong. I served for two years in the US Army, and I came to comprehend militaristic perspective. I quickly decided that I wanted no part of that mindset—unless, of course, it could be used, if necessary, in some subtle fashion that does not incur bodily harm to other living organisms, in intelligent defense of natural habitat and its denizens that have no other means of self-defense.

Habitats like the "Bears Ears" and the "Grand Staircase."

Indeed, the North American Southwest is the perfect geographic region in which to further biocentric ethical values. There remain vast areas of wild lands where rural populations are still in tune with the flow of Nature, who still celebrate the spirit of place, who honor habitat, who have not so "anthropo-centrified" their vision as to have become blinded to the nature of reality—or the reality of Nature.

It is quite clear that we have reached the stage in this still adolescent nation where federal legislation violates the principles of Nature. We are not alone. Our nation is one of many that continues to commit criminal acts against the biotic community. Here's the conundrum: When a nation designs legislation that defends criminal acts that are in obvious violation of ethical standards concerning the preservation of the biotic community, is one ethically wrong in breaking the law to defend the biotic communities that are being physically violated and endangered as the result of that federal legislation?

Or put another way, do we obey federal law or natural law?

To whom or what are we primarily accountable?

In his book, *The Practice of the Wild*, poet/environmental philosopher Gary Snyder wrote: "We must consciously fully accept that this is where we live and grasp the fact that our descendants will be here for millennia to come. . . . We must honor this land's great antiquity—its wildness—learn it—defend it—and work to hand it on to the children (of all beings) of the future with its biodiversity and health intact. . . . A worldwide purification of mind is called for: the exercise of seeing the surface of the planet for what it is—by nature. With this kind of consciousness people turn up at hearings and in front of trucks and bulldozers to defend the land or trees. Showing solidarity with a region! . . . Bioregionalism is the entry of place into the dialectic of history. Also we might say that there are "classes" which have so far been overlooked—the animals, rivers, rocks, and grasses—now entering history."

All of this contributes to the bioregional mindset—that of the naturist anarchist who is settling into his or her homeland with an expanded consciousness of one's own deep and abiding allegiance to homeland, to its biological, geophysical, and mythic characteristics of which we ourselves are part. Naturist anarchism is indeed democracy refined to its highest level. Naturist anarchism is bioregionalism put into practice. It is skinny-dipping in the flow of Nature with full recognition that we are but a tiny part of Nature's flow. Then while standing naked in the Sun in a state of Indigenous mindedness, we take stock of the current circumstances and react accordingly.

16. | Naturizing Consciousness

This essay originally appeared in Green Fire Times *(June 2018).*

TRY TO IMAGINE YOURSELF in a feral state, your mind wild, unfettered by complex language, legislation, or institutional bidding. Minutes and hours do not exist as such. Responding to hunger and thirst, maintaining vigilance, harmonizing with habitat—these are primary considerations. You are not stupid, but rather "wildly" intelligent, your intuition finely honed. You are loosely affiliated with others of your species with whom you cooperate at hunting and gathering food, banding together in mutual defense when necessary, procreating. Epoch-wise, you inhabit either the Pleistocene or post-Anthropocene—pre- or post-overshoot.

For anyone within range of this essay, it is impossible to fully imagine one's self in a state of feral consciousness. We are collectively too "anthropogenized"—dangerously de-naturized. Our consciousness is cluttered with the fruits of our success, just as our planet is overpopulated with our species. Only recently in our history have we revealed how tenuous our tenure as the dominant species has become. We are imploding for many reasons, not the least of which is the damage we have wrought within our planetary habitat. We have dangerously destabilized the home zone.

Big change is imminent.

I contend that if we really concentrate, we can partially restabilize and thus thwart total planetary disaster. But this will involve an entire paradigm shift to be accomplished within the human generation now coming into adulthood. In a word, it will take our children to save us from ourselves. It will take a revolution of planetary proportion.

The great Russian naturalist-anarchist Peter Kropotkin pointed out that social revolution can only be successful when the goal is a well-defined sustainable culture of practice. Kropotkin died a century ago when the human population of the planet had yet to number two billion. Today we are approaching eight billion and rising. We continue to dangerously over-extract natural resources as much of our population functions within a capitalist system of economics based on growth for its own sake. Political power is centralized within different nation states that compete for domination regardless of ecological consequences, thus our planet is rapidly becoming uninhabitable. Over a seventh of the human population is forced to live in poverty where food, water, sanitation, and overall living conditions are many degrees below substandard. While our population is growing, our livable habitat is shrinking. Only just now are many of us becoming aware that our planetary climate is changing, growing warmer due to excess carbon dioxide that is stifling the atmosphere, where the oceans, the soil and air themselves have all become a great dumping ground for the detritus of human overconsumption. As Wes Jackson points out, this is the most important moment in human history, even more important than our trek out of Africa many tens of thousands of years ago. For this is the historic moment where we either redefine and adjust our cultures of practice relative to the needs of our living planet, or we perish as one of many species for whom our planet has become inhospitable.

As a wise woman once said, the human species is like a giant meteor crashing into our living planet.

In a word, we have to change everything from the top down. And we have to do it from the bottom up.

Decentralization of Consciousness

My friend Jerry Mander once wrote a compelling book titled *Four Arguments for the Elimination of Television* wherein, among other things, he describes how beginning shortly after World War II, television came into national prominence and immediately caught the attention of virtually all Americans. In a later book, *The Capitalism Papers: Fatal Flaws of an Obsolete System*, he points out how corporate America commandeered the national psyche through television advertising and turned us into a nation committed to consumerism. The bottom line here is that after a sixteen-year period that included the Great Depression and WWII, we were ready to luxuriate in overabundance of artifacts that fulfilled our presumed needs. This came to dominate our national cultural perspective and was drilled into our collective consciousness through television advertising. That this overabundance of artifacts was wrought from limited natural resources was not a notion that came to prevail until decades later. Natural resources are extracted from the planet Earth and turned into money and throw-away artifacts. As time has passed, the corporate world subsumed the political world until now, we are governed by a political system—once intended to be democratic—that is presently held in sway by a corporate/military/industrial complex of such magnitude that we are into three generations of Americans whose primary focus is founded on economic growth for its own sake. In one of his most celebrated apothegms, author-anarchist Edward Abbey pointed out that "growth for the sake of growth is the ideology of the cancer cell."

As noted earlier, Ed also pointed out, "Freedom begins between the ears."

The latter posits a trail between the horns of the dilemma. Decentralize your mind away from the commons of human consciousness, a collective human perspective that is currently dominated by the corporate political oligarchy—and react according to your own interpretation of reality. How to do this? Don't watch the news for a day or a week or a month. Turn off your smart phone, go outside, find a patch of natural habitat, and observe, slowly letting that habitat fill your consciousness with the recognition that what we call Nature is our true source of life and consciousness. Indeed, the plants that grow, the insects that we see crawling along, the birds that cruise through the air overhead, are all distantly related to us, share genes with us—we're likely all descended from a common ancestor that popped into existence when our planet was young.

Indeed, our planet Earth that spawned us is alive. Our planet is part of the Solar System that includes the Sun, planets, satellites, meteors, comets, detritus—all comprised of elements, many of which scientists have identified that appear in the Periodic Chart, and probably others yet to be identified. Our Solar system is our greater home ecosystem that resides in space near the edge of our Milky Way Galaxy, itself but one of 200 billion or so galaxies in the known universe. There may be many more.

This helps put things in perspective. There are more galaxies in the universe than human beings who have lived and died on our planet Earth. Here we are, an animal species with the gift of evolved consciousness, and we have used that consciousness to bring ourselves (and many other species) to the very edge of extinction. Certainly we can do better than that. How about if we put the planet first, well before our presumed human needs, and devote ourselves to widespread, deep-rooted ecological restoration, even though it means bringing the corporate/political oligarchy to its knees as but one enormous ramification.

At this point, we dare not be too gradual. As far as climate change is concerned, some say we have thirty years to turn it around before the point of no return. Some say eleven years. Some think we may have already passed that point. Whatever the case, it would behoove us as a species to recentralize our focus on what absolutely needs to be done, and then do it, using whatever it takes.

Recentralization of Consciousness

Cynicism leads to leprosy of the soul whereas altruism leads to flowering of the spirit, or so I contend. Kropotkin forwarded the practice of mutual aid as a primary factor in the evolution of species as well as the evolution of human cultures. Mutual aid includes the practice of reciprocity. What I am urging here is that we as humans recognize the necessity to reciprocate with our planet Earth that spawned us and all other species over these last 3.8 billion years. In order for evolution to occur, our planet required that life and the elements—hydrogen, nitrogen, methane, oxygen, carbon, etc.—actively interact. They interact within ecosystems that are nested within larger ecosystems nested within even larger ecosystems until they are all reciprocally nested within the planetary ecosystem that is our planet Earth—which itself is a living system that interacts with the Sun. Wes Jackson recalls that his friend J. Stan Rowe pointed out that what every ecosystem has in common is contiguous volume. Living organisms on their own do not have contiguous volume. Ecosystems do whether they fit on the head of a pin or take up an entire planet. Our planet Earth is an ecosphere comprised of nested ecosystems in motion wherein life and its surrounding contiguous volume interact and foster more life. That is an amazing thought.

So here we are, the human species now numbering over 7.9 billion people on this planet better equipped to support a modest fraction of our current population. From the point of view of our planet the human species is committed to growth. Are we metastasizing, consuming everything in sight on our trail through time to satisfy our presumed human needs? That certainly seems to be the case. We have created countless institutions and passed endless legislation to justify our folly—namely, that we perceive ourselves as Nature's reason to be.

Wrong. Nature in all its complexity is its own reason to be. We humans are but one of Nature's countless quadrillions of experiments, one of uncounted millions and more species that evolved on our tiny planet Earth over nearly four billion years. We attained species-hood 200,000 to 300,000 years ago. We became *Homo sapiens*—pretty much who we are today—about 50,000 years ago. It took 10,000 generations for us to bring ourselves to the edge of extinction. We are the only species to have brought about a major spasm of extinction of species. On the other hand, sharks have been around for millions of years, and in the main, are doing well.

I personally acknowledge science as one of the greatest of human endeavors. In one sense, it is the practice of seeking irrefutable truth. Each branch of science seeks a bottom line in what makes the universe comprehensible. I have known many scientists, and I respect most of them. I have great difficulty in accepting corporate misapplication of science for economic growth at the endless expense of natural habitat. There is a meanness to us as a species that allows for disregard of life as we plunder and kill forests in order to grow hamburgers. Or daily dump thousands of tons of garbage into the oceans. Or stab this Earth with drilling rigs—"mother-frackers"—tapping into pockets of gas to burn or oil to pump. Or strip-mine many square miles of earth for coal. Or spew megatons of noxious fumes into the atmosphere. All of this damages each affected ecosystem, always disturbing natural balance, cumulatively edging fellow species into extinction.

Our cultural attention is inappropriately centralized. We are long overdue in recentralizing our individual and cultural attention on ecological balance on this beautiful planet Earth that spawned us and allows for our continued existence, at least for the time being . . .

17. | Seeking Coherence

This essay originally appeared in Green Fire Times *(August 2012).*

IN 1996, I HAD the opportunity to interview the eminent entomologist, Edward O. Wilson, in his office/laboratory at Harvard University. My friend Dan Curry and I were coproducing a video about cognitive diversity. Wilson's book, *Consilience*, had just been published, and the subject of his book certainly coincided with cognitive diversity.

Wilson's office/lab was an ant habitat with leafcutter ants carrying cut leaves back and forth along stalks of vegetation that extended from one terrarium to another. I was reminded that Edward O. Wilson was a world-class authority on ants.

Wilson defined his concept of "consilience" in the opening lines of our interview: "'Consilience' is not a new word. It goes back 160 years. It's got a nice sound to it, and it means literally 'a jumping together of knowledge' and specifically cause-and-effect explanations one discipline to the next. It's the driving force actually in the natural sciences. So you say that the explanations of physics are consilient in a cause-and-effect way with reagent chemistry, those with cell biology, those with evolutionary biology and neurobiology so to speak. The question before us in modern intellectual inquiry is, 'Are the social sciences and the humanities fundamentally consilient with the natural sciences?' And many of us think they are.

"Now, attention to consilience means attention to the methods that have triumphed in the natural sciences, not just reduction, the breaking down of complex systems into their elements and processes but the attempt to resynthesize from the knowledge of those elements and processes into a whole again. And when you can do reduction then follow it by synthesis as occurred in many of the physical science efforts, then you have the triumph of the natural sciences. So, consilience when successfully pursued, and as I'd like to see it all the way across the great branches of learning—natural sciences, social sciences, humanities—not only establishes and celebrates the fundamental unity of cause-and-effect explanations across all knowledge, but it also stimulates and connects up diversity of viewpoint and of acquisition of new knowledge."

Wilson went on to go into greater detail about consilience and cognitive diversity, but all expressed within the context of global academic culture even though Dan and I tried unsuccessfully to get him to consider something akin to the role of Indigenous mind in shaping a broader spectrum of human thought. Thus, for me, consilience from Wilson's perspective remains a highly intelligent but incomplete approach to what I've come to think of as coherent understanding.

Western science is a "culture of practice" comprised of many diverse specific disciplines whose common thread is pursuit of provable knowledge that cannot be refuted. Indeed, the pursuit of science is a fundament of global culture, a cornerstone of modern civilization. That science clashes with systems of belief such as fundamentalist religion reveals a realm of "conflicting absolutes" that defies cultural resolution. Science, or evidence-based knowledge, and belief-based religious institutional rote will remain at loggerheads until humankind refines its collective consciousness to integrate science, intuition of the Great Mystery, and coherence of collective mind recognizing that we are a member species of an evolving biotic community that inhabits a living planet, and that if indeed we have a purpose, evolution of consciousness lies at the heart of it.

———

OVER THE LAST half-century as an aural historian, I've followed my microphones throughout the western United States and Mexico as far south as Chiapas. This is the patch of our planet Earth that I dearly love, a large mosaic of habitats that contains an enormous amount of biodiversity, cultural diversity, and cognitive diversity, fertile turf for one who remains endlessly fascinated even after many decades of deep listening to the ever-murmuring mystery of existence.

The Seri Indians of Sonora, though influenced by global monoculture, remain hunter-gatherers fishing the Sea of Cortez, gathering edible native plants, and hunting wild game. Their songs reflect their profound understanding of topography and species native to their homeland, their mythic history, the shamanic prowess revealed by gifted members of their community.

On one occasion I visited my Seri friend, Jesús Rojo Montaño, in his cottage in Punta Chueca, Sonora, to record part of his repertoire of traditional songs. He told me in Spanish that he was going to sing the song of the leafcutter ant. He sat in front of my microphones and began to assume an entirely different countenance. Although he was still embodied in human form, he had become a leafcutter ant. He sang the Seri ant song four times, and when he was finished, after a period of fifteen or twenty seconds he gradually regained his humanness.

By now, I've witnessed this shape-shifting phenomenon on different occasions while recording Seri Indians and others. The music is sung from within a trancelike state wherein the singer is literally empowered by the subject of the song. The Seri singer who knows the complete repertoire of animal songs has an uncanny understanding of the regional fauna. Over a period of a dozen years, I've recorded several different musical forms of Seri music including what I call geomythic mapping songs wherein the singer recalls a point in the landscape and extols its characteristics both natural and supernatural. By knowing the entire repertoire of geomythic mapping songs, the singer has a multidimensional map of homeland and seascape embedded in her or his psyche. For the Seris, their mythic process and their shamanic practices bind them to homeland and explain their presence within the flow of Nature. The force of the Seri shamanic mind is formidable. To relegate this profound perspective of Indigenous mind to an abandoned meander is a crime against the flow of Nature.

The Colorado Plateau is a biogeographical province that is situated north of the Sonoran Desert. It contains a most intricate system of canyons and is regarded by many as one of the most beautiful places on Earth. It is home to many Indigenous cultures including the Ute Indians, the Navajo Indians, and the Hopis whose villages are situated on the three southern promontories of Black Mesa, a deeply sacred landform that lies in the heart of the Colorado Plateau.

Lyle Balenquah is a Hopi man who is both a trained archaeologist and a traditional culture-bearer whose perspective is invaluable as he gazes into the deep past to prehistoric cultures whose ruins provide major insights into the relationship of culture to habitat.

"We're all a part of these landscapes whether we're Hopi or Anglo or Walapai or Navajo or Zuni. We all have impacts in some ways on these landscapes. . . . Chaco Canyon has been used as a prime example of landscape change initiated by human interaction on a wide scale and how the impacts that prehistoric populations were having on the landscape led to their demise, so to speak. What can we learn from that and how do we view our place in the world today, and are we going to learn from those lessons of the past?

"I think that one of the things that Hopi stresses in a lot in our teachings is that there are a lot of good things that came from our ancestral history, a lot of positive values and philosophical ways of thinking. But there are also some negative lessons that we have to own up to. We have to take responsibility for them. Hopi history has both good and negative sides to it, and how are we going to maintain the good, the positive? We have to remember the . . . negative aspects of our history that will teach us today.

"How are we as modern Hopis and as a society going to interact with our environment? For me that's where culture as part of home-land comes in. I get to see this huge landscape across the Southwest. I get to see how prehistoric peoples were living in landscapes two, three, four hundred miles separated. But they all had to understand that they had to live within their means to some degree. And in some instances, they didn't live within their means and that caused turmoil, that caused chaos, that caused things to go wrong for themselves, for their society. You tie all of that together, you bring all of these different examples within the Southwest of prehistoric cultures experiencing good and bad changes and I think that's what Hopi is, is trying to remember. In our modern way of thinking, we're struggling to maintain those good positive things, and some people might not want to remember the bad things, but I think we have to because those are the things that are going to teach us—not only this generation but those that are coming.

"So there's a lot tied into that idea of culture as part of homeland. What is the common foundation that we all have to live by?"

While we are shaped in part by the habitat we select as homeland, we are also shaped by how we choose to comport ourselves. Science in its various disciplines provides an adventure of extraordinary magnitude for its practitioners. But science is not the only culture of practice that exists within the sphere of human consciousness.

I have learned an enormous amount from my traditional Indian friends over the last sixty years. Perhaps the most profound knowledge that has been imparted to me is that to secularize thence commoditize land and water is wrong-minded. I have also learned that cultural attitude, collective will, is a part of consciousness and that unless cultural attitude is deeply aligned with a sense of being kindred with all fellow creatures, with our sustaining planet, we are collectively awry. We are out of balance with the flow of Nature. My traditional Indian friends invariably understand this. Indigeneity to homeland greatly strengthens that sense of being kindred, that intuition of the sacred nature of life and consciousness as well as the mystery of existence.

Metaphorically, human consciousness peers through a vast crystal of many windows, and just as the Sun's ray casts a rainbow hue, so does human consciousness portend an extraordinary evolving coherence of potential.

18. | Lingering Speculations

THIS MORNING, I RETURNED from my daily walk through the piñon-juniper grassland that has been my home habitat for six decades. I inhaled from the soft wind (*p'o-wa-ha*), greeted the land, and let its mystique flow through me. I marveled at the orange-vermillion beauty of the six Indian paintbrush flowers that grow just west of our adobe home in the high country. As I stood there, a brown towhee landed on top of my head startling me, then flew off to the nearby grandfather juniper tree that lives about thirty feet beyond the western wall of our home. I was gratified that the towhee had not shat in my hair.

A wildfire of over 700 acres currently burns atop the Jemez Mountains thirty-five miles to the northwest. The wind blows from the north casting the smoke-plume to the south just high enough that beneath it I can faintly see Mt. Taylor, known to the Navajos as Tzootsil, a 10,000-foot-high mountain that is situated about a hundred miles to the west near the southeastern edge of the Colorado Plateau.

The Colorado Plateau is separated from another plateau that stretches like a drumhead southward from the southern promontories of the Rocky Mountains drained by the Río Grande, or O-son-geh, in the language of the Tewa speaking Puebloan Indians, who have lived along its banks for centuries.

This is Indian Country populated by peoples of different cultures that have evolved here since the beginning of the warming trends of the Holocene, since their antecedents began migrating into this region before the end of the last Ice Age, the Pleistocene epoch, when the elements frosted the now toasted landscape. These so-called "Indian" cultures evolved as their respective habitats, their home ecosystems, settled into the Holocene epoch. Their cultural perspectives were shaped by their mindful observations of the flora and fauna, the weather patterns, the aridity of homeland, as well as their intuitions fed by rootedness in the flow of Nature that sculpted their mythic coordinates that provided their reasons to be.

"All these lands, when you look at them, . . . the landscape has a memory, only we have forgotten what that memory is. So we have to go back and rediscover that memory. That's one of the things that I've been doing. Like here in my place I discovered that there were terraces here that apparently my grandfather had done. But when I moved here, of course my grandfather died in 1935, so I never knew any of my grandfathers because like I said, I was the youngest of my family. But probably because of being the youngest, I always would think to myself, *I wonder what my grandfathers were like?* I would really have liked to have been able to sit down like we're sitting down here and talk with them about the land." So said my late, great friend, Estevan Arellano, a Hispano culture-bearer who lived in Embudo near the banks of the Río Embudo, a tributary of the Río Grande. We sat beneath an apricot tree fingering potshards left in the wake of passing Pueblo Indians who had camped here in earlier centuries. Indeed, the land has a memory, some of which is still captured in cultural recollection of humans whose ancestors drank from the waters of O-son-geh when my own ancestors were reshaping the spirit of place in the Old World (Europe) into a jealous transcendental god now long removed from Nature.

As noted earlier, Ed Abbey once said, "I think that the Indians and most traditional cultures had a much wiser point of view in that they invested every aspect of the world around them—all of Nature— animal life, plant life, the landscape itself with gods, with deity. In other words, everything was divine in some way or another. Pantheism probably led to a much wiser way of life, more capable of surviving over long periods of time."

Indeed, pantheism does lead to a more complete understanding of our place in Nature that in turn leads to levels of cultural comportment that we have too long neglected, that we have too long forgotten. It is not superstition to recognize the divine in Nature, especially as one recognizes that consciousness is spawned by life, at least on this planet. Science is a greater culture of practice committed to seeking and understanding irrefutable truth. I am not trained in science, but I recognize that it has contributed to our conscious understanding enormously, and I am grateful for its practitioners who seek the truth pursuing time-tested paths of inquiry. Less than a year before this writing, certain cosmologists and astronomers cautiously upped the presumed population of galaxies in the known universe from 200 billion to a couple of trillion. That's roughly twenty galaxies for every human who has lived on our planet, Earth. Our galaxy, the Milky Way, has as many as 200 billion suns. It swirls away through a universe thought to have popped into being about 13.7 billion solar years ago. Quantum physicists currently contemplate the possibility of up to an infinite number of universes that coexist. How large is infinitely large? How small is infinitely small?

Biologists suggest that there may be as many as ten million species presently alive on our planet Earth. But how many species have existed since LUCA, the last universal common ancestor, began contributing to our gene pool nearly four billion years ago, LUCA whose genetic imprint is ostensibly still to be found in every species now known, our kindred life forms?

That grandfather juniper tree outside my studio window is a faraway cousin, a distant relative too precious to convert into firewood. Maybe my own bones will feed his roots in the not-too-distant future.

Some years before his death, my friend Stewart Udall and I were sipping wine in the early evening afterglow beneath the portal at his home in the foothills of the Sangre de Cristo Mountains outside Santa Fe. "Jack," he said, "we must never lose sight of the Great Mystery." Neither of us ever did.

It's been well over a half-century since my friend Stewart Brand asked me to participate in a project called *America Needs Indians*. It was shortly thereafter that I was invited by a family of very traditional Navajos to move into a forked-stick hogan a couple hundred yards away from their family cluster of hogans at Navajo Mountain in the northern reaches of the Navajo Reservation. We shared no common language, but we became friends. It was there that I "osmosed" some cultural understanding and came to realize how much their cultural perspective was shaped by their home habitat in the heart of the Colorado Plateau. I have had absolutely no academic training in anthropology, and at that time was just beginning to try my hand at the practice of aural history, which has been much of my lifeway ever since. It was there that I first listened to songs sung by *hataali*, or medicine men, songs passed down through the generations, and said to be learned from the *yei'is*, or spirit beings, that continue to prevail in crannies hidden within the Colorado Plateau.

Since then, I have befriended and often lived with Indigenous peoples from Southern Ute, Hopi, Navajo, Tewa, Keresan, Tiwa, Nez Perce, Warm Springs, Tohono O'odham, Pima, Yaqui, Chiricahua Apache, Shoshone, Paiute, Seri, Huichol, and Tarahumara cultures throughout the American West and Mexico. I've recorded songs and stories from most of these cultures and have thus received an education that could never have been gained in any institution. I have also recorded Hispano culture in the North American Southwest, a culture now Indigenous to this region after twenty generations of rooting itself into the soil of New Mexico. At least as important as any recording is the level of friendship that I now experience with so many people who have shared their perspectives with me through story and song. I have also recorded the habitat itself, and now attune my ear to where I camp anywhere in this immense region of extreme beauty, arid harshness, and geophysical, biological, and cultural diversity. I can look at John Wesley Powell's map of the watersheds of the arid West and picture them in my mind's eye and hear them in my mind's ear because I have visited almost all of them and hearkened to their common message—that every habitat is sacred in some universal sense, and each has helped shape myriad levels of living cognition, including cultural consciousness that contribute to a commons of human consciousness that is now endangered by much of our human species having gone awry.

The practice of aural history is not yet a science, but rather (in my case) an almost desperate endeavor to record endangered perspectives without which broader understanding is left bereft. After a very long lifetime at large on this exquisite planet, I see my role as gathering seeds of Indigenous perspective to hopefully be replanted within the commons of human consciousness. Without hearkening to that Indigenous perspective that mainstream monoculture has all but annihilated, we shall have spent our collective consciousness, this great gift of life, in pursuit of the paltry. We can do better than this, but there is so little time and very little political inclination.

Advice is dangerous, but so is extinction of species, including our own. So, I say, use your imagination, listen to your homeland, hearken back to the utterances of those traditional people Indigenous to this continent, and react. Look at legislation that runs counter to the flow of Nature and counteract it. Practice civil disobedience to the extent that your personal system of ethics allows. Organize watershed by watershed, as defined by John Wesley Powell, and disavow the geopolitical boundaries imposed by federal government. Invigorate grassroots governance and polycentric governance as espoused by Elinor Ostrom. Look up the meaning of polycentric governance if you don't already know what it means. Rethink economics with ecological perspective as the dominant cultural characteristic and oust the "money kings" from political power. Contribute to the reshaping of collective cultural attitude that is in harmony with the natural world. Remember that the planet is a commons available to all species, the extinction of any of which lessens the commons. And come to understand that we all participate in the commons of human consciousness and that each of us is responsible for what we allow to prevail in our own minds. De-secularize habitat and re-sacralize homeland.

And here I reiterate the recorded words of my late, great friend, Rina Swentzell, a Tewa Indian woman from the Santa Clara Pueblo:

"Trees are living beings. Rocks are living beings. Water. The spirit moves through the water. An incredible word that we have for the source of life is something that we talk about as the *p'o-wa-ha*. The water-wind-breath. It is there in the water and in the wind that we can see the spirit, that we can see life moving, there where the life force is visible. As well as in the clouds, of course. We don't take the life force and put it in a superhuman being, as Christians do with God. That already begins to show us the focus on humans, and human beings. When you put the life force in a super-human creature, God is in superhuman form. But we [Puebloans] keep it [Spirit] within the trees, within the water, within the wind, within the clouds. And we are to move through that context, with the water, the wind, and breathe the same breath. To say 'we are breathing the same breath that the rocks do, that the wind does'—that gives you a totally different feeling. This is it. There is no other reality. We don't go to heaven. We don't leave this dirty world to go to a golden clean heaven. We are here. This is it. This is the world. It doesn't get any better than this. And if we don't honor it in the sense that this is the best, the most beautiful as it is ever going to be, then we can't take care of it if we think that it is a place to be shunned and that we have better things to look forward to. Then we can't walk respectfully where we are at this moment, and take care of things, and touch things with honor. And breathe each breath. That is what that 'water-wind-breath' is about. Because I mean, my goodness, here it is. And every second I can breathe it in, and become a part of this world, and know in no uncertain terms, I am a part of this world that I live in every second—I believe it every second."

Conclusion

Invigorating Metamorphosis

This essay originally appeared in The Gulch *(2021).*

IT'S TOUGH TO OVERCOME inertia, especially when it is self-imposed by presumed limitations. I speak from experience as a mid-point octogenarian having survived the last fourteen months of pandemic living in relative isolation from my fellow humans. For someone who has been a self-employed documentary radio producer and writer for many years, solitude remains a hallmark of existence, a domain treasured for private reflection and hopefully, creative thought. However, isolation enforced by the determination to remain out of virus-ridden harm's way casts a different spin on one's perception of solitude.

I neither watch nor listen to the news, nor do I partake of social media in this age where virtual reality has all but subsumed the real McCoy. But I do scan the headlines in either the *New York Times* or *Guardian* on my computer a couple times a week. And be-masked, I cast my vote in person during the last general election. Indeed, I was escorted to the front of the queue by a voter's assistant who recognized that I'm an elder and must thus be treated accordingly. I was grateful that she didn't thereafter put me out to pasture. That's my own prerogative. Nonetheless, inertia born of nonactivity has brought me mighty close to glimpsing that westward trail into the sunset.

However, the flow of Nature has carried me through many rapids as I row my way through my decades. Running rivers in my own raft has inspired an enduring metaphor of my lifetime. I've learned that failing to pay heed can lead to disaster. Getting caught in an eddy is just such a showstopper if one fails to work relentlessly to get back into one's natural flow. To be alive includes recognition of the nature of the unexpected and responding consciously.

My generation of monocultural Americans has fostered overindulgence. I can't exclude myself even though I criticize this collective failing that has brought our geo-biotic community to a possibly fatal impasse. "Head 'em off at the impasse!" shouted Ed Abbey as we contemplated a clouded future forty years ago. His was an unrelenting vigor cut short by biological circumstance too few years after that utterance. He didn't get to be an old man. But I sure did, and I can tell you that the rapids of old age spark realizations that must be addressed lest one sink into the fatal eddy of inertia.

I've spent much of my long life recording personal and cultural perspectives revealed by a particularly diverse array of humans and other fellow creatures throughout southwestern North America, my favorite patch of paradise. I may possibly have come to glean some miniscule sense of the enormity of diversity spawned by the flow of Nature on our planet Earth. I'm comfortable with the hypothesis forwarded by Humberto Maturana that life and cognition are two intermingled aspects of the same phenomenon. I ponder the relevance of this with regard to the process of biological evolution on our planet Earth. I realize that cultural evolution occurs far more rapidly than biological evolution, at least within our human species, and possibly many other species due in part to the enormous impact we humans are engendering on the eco-region that is our planet. After reading essays by Lynn Margulis (who codeveloped the Gaia Hypothesis with James Lovelock), I have come to intuit the importance of symbiosis in evolution. The great anarchist-scientist Peter Kropotkin was of the opinion that evolution of species including our own owes far more to mutual cooperation than mutual antagonism.

I've listened to people of many diverse Indigenous cultures, and while their creation myths may differ in storyline, the fundamental truth that life and land are sacred remains part of a prevailing motif.

And while there is an enormous amount to admire in the "techno-logic" of Western culture, the bigger perspective eludes too many of us. It was just sixty years ago while having a peyote vision in a rural setting on Mount Tamalpais in Marin County that I came to realize the necessity of "pulling all the nails out of my frame of reference" and opening my consciousness to the myriad revelations spawned by the flow of Nature. Subsequently, I sincerely try to remain in the center of an ever-expanding sphere of reference functioning within the limitations of my own consciousness.

Katherine, my wife of half a century, and I inhabit a house built of adobe bricks situated in the middle of a twelve-acre span of piñon-juniper grassland also populated with cholla cactus, yucca, dwarf chamisa, assorted grasses, and occasional wildflowers, including Indian paintbrush and primrose. We own the deed but not the land. No one can own land. We do little to affect the land, rather observing it restore itself year by year according to its own nature. It was overgrazed by cattle in a preceding century. Now is a time of extended drought. Aridity is the prevailing characteristic. It is our homeland, and we are part of the wildlife. Or we try to be in spite of having been culturally formatted into consumers no longer capable of hunting and gathering as practiced by our Pleistocene ancestors, nor engaging in self-sustaining agriculture as did many of our grandparents and their immediate forbears. Yet we do our best to live frugally. I'm astounded that in my eighty-five years of life, the human population of the planet has grown from about 2.2 billion in 1936 to 7.9 billion as of May 2021.

As I write, a turkey vulture circles overhead. Not yet, old friend. I'm still busy. Busy? Doing what? I'm attempting to re-wild my consciousness, not yet ready to become food for vultures and coyotes and other less delectable critters by human standards. I'm still marinating, spicing up my consciousness in a whole-hearted attempt to digest the realization that I am spawned by this Earth, that I belong to the fabric of this Earth, that indeed I am an Earthling who has spent most of my life seeking to undam the flow of Nature through human consciousness, ever-abandoning unnecessary meanders into stagnant eddies of soul-debilitating pursuits. I love this planet Earth with an abiding passion. I seek to re-wild my consciousness in order to restore my intuitive understanding of how best to comport myself as a latter-day natural being.

Have I figured out how best to do this? Only tentatively. First, I have to adapt to circumstances. It used to be that I could happily hike ten or fifteen miles daily wearing a backpack immersing myself in distant canyons, following game trails, looking for hidden springs, otherwise dancing in Paradise. Or running rivers springtime water fresh flush with roiling rapids, or extended spans of calm water inducing serenity enhanced by the thrill of hearing the downward slurring song of the canyon wren, to me one of the most poignant and beautiful of Nature's sounds. Thus, I pursued many adventures with my aforementioned compañero for decades until he died and disappeared somewhere out there in no-man's land.

I have sought Nature's truths by wandering afield with recorder and microphones, recording songs and perspectives of Indigenous tribal members whose knowledge of homeland is imbedded in cultural music and lore and reveals deeper truths than found elsewhere, truths that unveil intuitive understandings by virtue of shared cognition with osprey, deer, the leafcutter ant. Indeed, this practice has provided me my formal education, formal in the sense that it has always been with great formality and genuine respect that I have approached these peoples who have responded in kind by sharing their understandings and cultural wisdom born of recognizing that they are themselves part of their homeland. This is deep intuitive understanding that is mightily profound and natural. Like breathing or drinking.

Robert A. Heinlein coined the word *grok* that appears in his superb novel published in 1961, *Stranger in a Strange Land.* Grok is not a beautiful word, but it wended its way into the Oxford English Dictionary and is summarized as such: "to understand intuitively or by empathy, to establish rapport with; to empathize or communicate sympathetically (with); also, to experience enjoyment." Thus, traditional "Indigenes" that I have come to know, and many whom I have befriended, grok their homeland, the nature of their fellow creatures, their own place in Nature. This has had a profound influence on me and has commanded my abiding respect for Indigenous mindedness.

Now that I am old, rickety, and wrinkled, I've since parted ways with my backpack and raft. I still walk a half, three-quarters or even a mile almost every morning, just to keep a foot in, so to speak. Our rural homeland is less rural than it was a quarter-century ago, but it still harbors wildlife. We put out water for the birds, coyotes, and bobcats. I remain fascinated as I look through the window of my studio at different species who take their turn at the "watering hole." Some species of birds share water concurrently. Red-shafted flickers don't chase off the mountain bluebirds, while robins are very territorial even within their species. The Bendire's thrasher hops into the water, splashes with great vigor, and then jumps to the edge of the birdbath, shaking away water like a dog. It's a real thrill when a Cooper's hawk comes by for a drink. Chihuahuan ravens frequently soak scavenged morsels of food in the water to tenderize them. Ravens are very intelligent, having as many as 200 different vocalizations available in their linguistic repertoire.

I spend a fair amount of time watching ants, trying to grok their perspectives. As I mentioned in an earlier chapter, I once interviewed Edward O. Wilson in his office at Harvard University and was inspired to see two terraria situated side by side with long-stalked plants looping from one terrarium to the other. Leafcutter ants used these plant stalks to bridge the span. It was fascinating. Wilson was regarded as a leading authority on ants and has traveled the world as an ant watcher. I wistfully wish that he could have met my late Seri Indian friend who sang the song of the leafcutter ant while assuming the characteristics of the ant. Maybe that would have expanded Wilson's sense of consilience.

I'm fascinated by snakes of which we have neighboring bull snakes, red racers, and the occasional prairie rattlesnake. I'm very careful to move any rattler into my ice chest, never harming it physically. I drive a dozen or so miles down the highway and release it into a countryside less likely to be trekked over by humans. I know I'm messing with the rattler's sense of geography but rather that than endanger occasionally visiting kith and kin, or the snake itself.

I watch the sky almost every night. I've twice noted that May 6 is my last time to see the constellation Orion disappear into the afterglow of sunset before he reappears in early autumn. The farthest I can see with the naked eye is the Andromeda galaxy 2.5 million light years from here. It's harder to see than some years ago when the air was less murky and light pollution less pronounced. It's predicted that the Andromeda and Milky Way Galaxies will collide in four or five billennia.

These are some of the ways I try to re-wild my current state of consciousness. My eye knows the surrounding horizon intimately. I endlessly ponder weather patterns. Watching clouds is a pastime. If asked if I'm of a particular persuasion I reply that I'm simply a naturist. I try to imagine life during the Pleistocene. One of my favorite books is *Coming Home to the Pleistocene* by Paul Shepard. Another is *Desert Solitaire* by Edward Abbey. And yet another is *The Practice of the Wild* by Gary Snyder.

Now, as we tentatively approach a turning point in this time of pandemic, I look back and realize that I haven't wasted my time sitting outside grokking the flow of Nature passing through the present moment or watching birds through my studio window or walking, limping a bit through my morning saunters, or reading poetry or even snoozing. This is who I am. This is what it is to be an elder who continues to advocate on behalf of our planet Earth.

Wow—there went a hummingbird! And that old buzzard has moved on. Life is still good here on planet Earth.

Acknowledgments

The essays in this anthology were written over a period of fifty years. However, all but two have been written since the turn of the twenty-first century. Many of them were published in the *Green Fire Times* in Santa Fe, New Mexico, by editor and publisher Seth Roffman. Seth has worked indefatigably for decades to both plant and nurture "seeds of change" and has cast light on the deeply intertwined relationship between biodiversity and cultural diversity.

Other publications wherein some of these essays appeared include *El Palacio*, the publication of the Museum of New Mexico; *Clear Creek*, "the environmental viewpoint" of a half-century past; *Wild Earth*, the publication of the Wildlands Project; *The Gulch* from Durango, Colorado; and *Earth Island Journal* from Berkeley, California. To all these fine publications I am grateful.

And many thanks are due to my old friend of over six decades, Yvonne Bond, who transcribed scores of my recorded interviews, some of which have been excerpted for this anthology.

I express my gratitude with deep humility to the hundreds of people of many cultural persuasions whose perspectives I've recorded over nearly sixty years and who have provided my true education.

Mil gracias to my many friends at the University of New Mexico Press who have seen fit to publish my books over the decades.

Finally, I am profoundly grateful to the spirit of Nature for allowing me to have a consciousness, endless curiosity, unbounded enthusiasm, a taste for adventure, and deep love for our planet Earth. Skinny-dipping in the flow of Nature is a daily delight available to us all.

Thank you.